How I found my
True Inner Peace

How I found my
True Inner Peace

Book 1

by
Maggie Anderson

BALBOA
PRESS

A DIVISION OF HAY HOUSE

Balboa Press books may be ordered through
booksellers or by contacting:

Balboa Press
A Division of Hay House
1663 Liberty Drive
Bloomington, IN 47403
www.balboapress.com
1-(877) 407-4847

ISBN: 978-1-4525-3824-2 (sc)
ISBN: 978-1-4525-3825-9 (e)
Library of Congress Control Number: 2011915542

Printed in the United States of America

Balboa Press rev. date: 09/14/2011

Contents

 In Gratitude

I'd like to thank and dedicate this book to the Divine God/Goddess who sparked me into expressing on paper what is inside of me. This book is, also, lovingly dedicated to Kwan Yin, Mother Mary, the Angels, ArchAngels, Ascended Masters and higher beings, as well as to all those who have inspired me to write this book and finish it. Thank you so much to my Husband, Don, who lovingly and tirelessly assisted me in reviewing and editing. And I offer my utter gratitude and appreciation to the many masters along my path that have contributed to the expression of this book. To list a few: writings and energy from Eckhart Tolle, Kim Engh, Dr. Wayne Dyer, Doreen Virtue, Denise Linn, Abraham-Hicks, Matt Kahn, Panache Desai, Maureen Moss, Joan Wood, Chrism, Louise L. Hay, Oprah and the beautiful yoga Sadhana & upliftments from Shiva Rea, Seane Corn, Denise Austin, as well as Chalene Johnson and sooo many more that I can't list here that have crossed my path.

How I Found My
TRUE INNER PEACE

BOOK 1

Introduction

"**Y**ou're so weird. Nobody else would ever say that to me, *ever*!" my Husband exclaimed. He asked how my day was going and I told him my day was going great as I had just finished doing some yoga in a bathroom stall at work. Gotta be me! Okay, just to clarify, I work for a very nice corporate company that keeps their bathrooms immaculate. Not to mention, when I practice yoga in a bathroom stall, it's usually in a rarely used bathroom. And yes, I do wash my hands. :) So I thanked my Husband because I'm happy to be weird! Why be like everyone else. It's not entirely possible even though we can pretend. We are each unique beings having a unique experience.

We each have a Divine Spark within us. Embracing the Divine fire within you causes transformations that change you forever. It is beautiful and powerful. It enables you to discover that the Divine is everywhere—that there is no place the Divine is not. The Divine is all around us. The Divine is within you! The Divine is within me. My hope in writing this book is to help you find your divinity within—your true inner self.

The ideas I will share with you are not new, but ancient wisdom that have come to my consciousness. We each have this inner truth and can tap into it at any time. You will read about awakening to a higher awareness of who you are, empowering yourself through conscious awareness of your mental surroundings and living in the present. It is a journey inward for truth, peace and wisdom. It is how I have been guided to live my life with the tools that will get you there too.

With *How I found my True Inner Peace* it is my intention that it assists you in learning to find your true inner peace. All while assisting you in living your every day life in the flow. If your goal is to happily live a more conscious, authentic, awakened, joy-filled life, you will find guidance within this book. I share only the ideas that have come to me of raising consciousness for living an enlightened life. These ideas are not new but ancient concepts that have come to my consciousness to share with you. You will learn how to empower yourself through conscious awareness of your surroundings and what you create in every moment! Dive in and feel the wonderful powerful shifts within. And as you follow your inner hearts guidance system with clarity your unique path opens up to you.

Now is the time. If you're reading this, it's likely that right now you are ready to embrace something deeper within yourself. You are ready to awaken the mystery and blossom like a lotus. Keep in mind, however, that truth lies within. You cannot find your truth in a book. Although books may guide and uplift, they can lead you only to the point of your own discovery that the answers are always—and always have been—right there within you. The truth lies within. It is my intention that this remembrance occurs for everyone and you are empowered to share your essence.

Therefore, as you read this book, let yourself be lifted up, embrace whatever helps you along your journey into Self, and leave the rest. There is so much I still do not know and so much I know I am still only just now learning. I am simply sharing what I have come to at this point in my journey. Take what you like and leave the rest.

How I found my True Inner Peace holds answers to many questions of real life expression, expansion and transcendence. I write this book, not just for you, but for myself. In writing *How I found my True Inner Peace* I am reminded of the lessons I've learned, the soul searching I went through and the lessons I am still learning. I've made mistakes. We all do. And we bless these mistakes that show us how we can correct it next time. While writing *How I found my True Inner Peace* I was reminded to take a step back and breathe; live for the blissful present moment. It is a conversation with myself and all of you who have helped me to help myself just by BEING. I thank you all from the depths of my heart.

Through my experiences it became clear that the true path to sharing light with the world is to first work on the Self. We must be totally aligned in the higher realms and resonate at that frequency. In moving from this sacred space within we can then share light with everyone. As you heal your life you give others permission to do the same. In this book you will learn the tools I was guided to use in order to do just that.

How I found my True Inner Peace was crafted through the powerful connection I received via the energy and love that poured through me as I vigorously typed away. This book is also shaped by my own personal experiences and the teachings from the many teachers in my life who have touched my heart, challenged me and assisted me in being the real me. Teachers like Eckhart Tolle, Buddha, Kwan Yin, and the many teachers from workshops I've attended, attunements I've received, books I've read, online learning's I've participated in, as well as the day to day teachers of my family, children, friends and many strangers. All of these teachers assisted me in who I have become, which is more of the true me that I always was. Forever learning and evolving, I offer this part of me as a guide for you. It is my intention that reading *How I found my*

True Inner Peace brings you more peace, energy renewal and conscious awareness in your life.

How I found my True Inner Peace is crafted as BOOK ONE in a two-part series that will lead you on your path to Enlightenment. As I wrote this book it became clear that the book be separated into two clear visions on their own that are linked with each other in a progression. In this first book, Part I, we dive deep into the Natural Laws of the Universe and in Part II we go deeper into the steps of How I Found My True Inner Peace. In the second book much of the sacred mechanics of our awakening is revealed and a deep look at daily devotions and healing the self is shared. Both books bring with them amazing transformations as you integrate the learnings held within.

In not wanting to confuse those who read this I wanted to explain when you hear me talk about our Light and the Universe. I use the word God and I use the word Divine a lot in this book. The two words are interchangeable for me. God is the Divine. And the Divine is God; the all encompassing energy cosmic consciousness of the All that Is. This is how it is for me and as you read, this become clearer for you as well.

You may choose to read this book from cover to cover as it is laid out. Or you can have some fun with the soul. You can ask your soul to open up to a page for a lesson you need to learn that day. Then simply open the book and see what messages await you. Have some fun with it!

What is Awakening?

Prior to diving into the depths of this book, it's important to define the terms awakening and ascension. As we learn to find our inner center and peaceful state of being we evolve and open ourselves up even more to the divine being that we are, or rather awaken. Ascension is the awakening to our true Divine Spirit—the Divine Spirit we have always been and are getting to know again. You are much more than your mind tells you that you are. When we are awakened, we are no longer asleep, rolling with the punches of life in the mass consciousness. We become awakened to life on a new and higher level. We become aware of the divine in all of us.

Ascension gives us a higher vantage point from which we see that we are evolving into a much more connected race that is transitioning into a new dimension. You are so much more than your mind tells you that you are. You can do and be and are so much more! Awareness and love comes from within, but rather we *are* awareness and we *are* love. We are the Divine and the Divine is us. The realization of this is awakening.

We see that life is miraculous at every turn. And not only that, we realize that we have the power within ourselves to make our life amazing. Ascension is the evolvement of Mother Earth and the Human Race. We are evolving into a much more finely-tuned connected race. We are energy beings and vibrate at different frequencies. We each have a frequency, as does Mother Earth. As these frequencies rise up we become more of the higher beings we've always been. We become awakened to life on a new and higher level. We are moving into a new dimension. Essentially, ascension is the constant releasing of the old (all that has been created before) and the bondage of the ego, while opening up to your true Divine Self. We are all Divine and we are aligning more with remembering our pure Divine Soul.

It is happening now. No one is left behind. Some are already awakened and some are in the process of awakening and again some will soon go through the major changes that allow the process to go through them as well. The time is only Now.

We each have a divine spark within us that is our core essence and our core essence is Love. Our ego's or personalities cloak our true essence. It is hiding our true selves. Our ego is here to serve us while in this reality and not the other way around. Somewhere along the way the ego took over and we are slaves to it. As we awaken we will tame that beast. As we ascend we release more and more of our ego's hold and the filter of our personalities. We, thus, show more of our true selves. Our true nature is peace. By bringing peace to ourselves we bring it to the world. As each of us align with our Higher

Selves, our Light Body, our true Divine essence, we create a synergy of that light consciousness within that awakens and blossoms out to reach the depths of all souls. The seed has already been planted and now we are blooming. It is time.

We eventually transmute our "lower" selves as we awaken and ascend and take on more of our "higher selves" and bring that guidance and light more and more within us. This brings the guidance clearer and stronger in our heart. In either way we always have this guidance and sometimes it takes a quiet moment to truly hear our true heart and soul and its guidance. Check in with your heart. You can do this even without meditating or years of practice. It's always been there; ongoing, all the time. Can you feel it? Guidance is ongoing, simply getting present gets you there. Get present in every moment and your heart voice is heard loud and clear.

Everyone is special and all of us have the gifts. Everyone can do this. Everyone can remove their own blockages for powerful healing. You have it. You can work towards it. In these ascension times it is our expansion of consciousness that is bringing us all to this expanded way of living and being.

To understand the mechanics of awakening it is important to briefly explain our energy bodies and Kundalini. For the purpose of this book I am including only a snippet of information about these inner workings and do elaborate at length the larger picture in the second part of this two-part series, *Divine Embrace*.

Our energy bodies are made up of a yin and yang, a male and female half. Each halves making a whole. We can't have one without the other. Each makes up the other. For many many years we've been heavily in our male halves. The Divine Feminine energies are now emerging to complete the other half in a balanced connection. As the two merge together, we become one whole being. Shiva is our masculine side and Shakti our feminine. However, they are one in the same really. We merge these together and realize it's always been both and not just one over the other. As Shiva Rea likes to say, "What is the mover behind the mover."

In our energy bodies we have seven main energy vortices or Chakras (out of hundreds of chakras) that align along the center of our body from the base of our spine all the way up to the crown of our heads. (More on chakras later.) Surrounding these chakras are three main Nadi's (out of 72,000 nadi's) called the Ida, Pingala and Sushumna. The Ida nadi is our left side of the body that goes from our left nostril to mid-brain all the way down to the left perineum. Ida holds the energy qualities of feminine, lunar, cooling and passive. The Pingala nadi is our right side of the body located in our right nostril to mid-brain and all the way down to the right perineum. The Pingala holds masculine, sun, heating, active energy qualities. The Ida and Pingala wrap around the seven main chakras looking seemingly like DNA strands or like two serpents rising up to the crown of our heads. Where they join is a chakra. The Sushumna nadi goes from the base of our spine straight up along the spine and all the way up through the crown of our heads (or Crown Chakra).

Sushumna is the Kundalini life force energy, also known as Spiritual Energy, even Serpent power. We all possess this wide unknown, yet powerful creative energy life-force of Kundalini.

During this process we clear our energy blocks within our energy centers (chakras and aura). Or rather Kundalini assists in the clearing via energy surges and experiences. Kundalini pierces the energy centers (chakras) as it rises and will continue to rise up as it works on any old past patterns and blockages that may come up through the rising of our Kundalini energy. As this happens a Kundalini awakening occurs that may or may not be smooth in its process. Kundalini rides up the spine seemingly like two snakes electrically charged flowing from the Root chakra all the way up to the Crown chakra. Now if Kundalini hits a blockage it will stay there while working on that blockage but it does not stop at one chakra till that is cleared. It will continue to work simultaneous on other chakras. It works in succession with other chakras for clearing. It will only give you what you can and are meant to handle. Some will have a smoother balanced ride and others are destined to have a wild ride. Kundalini is a lifetime experience. It does not stop with one nifty experience and you're awakened, enlightened and all done. No, it goes on for a lifetime of experiences, even after awakened you will still go through your normal life. As the saying goes before enlightenment you chop wood and carry water. After enlightenment you chop wood and carry water; only maybe with more joy, presence and awareness.

The purpose of Kundalini awakenings is the preparation for your mind, body and soul in reaching the expanded state of consciousness. You will come to learn that it helps for a better way of being to keep your energy moving, never growing stagnant. Stagnancy is the only true death we may ever experience. Growing stagnant allows for built up emotions, negativity, complacency and ego to rule your unconscious living. Our bodies are transforming and the Kundalini awakening is assisting this to occur. If the body is prepared beforehand with a healthy lifestyle and healthy living, then the rising Kundalini will leave with it a balanced transformation over a balanced timeframe that is unique to each individual. If not, the rising is disturbing and sometimes painful for days, weeks or years (such as in Gopi Krishna's case as told in his book *The Awakening of Kundalini*). Kundalini's spark of life force will assist you in cleaning up your life in all ways. So the Kundalini spark assists with the spiritual awakening.

If we have blockages and ignore the signs or experiences that are trying to assist us in releasing those blockages (releasing through experiences, meditation, Higher Self or Angelic guidance) our Kundalini awakening will feel downright awful and take longer than need be. These blockages are karma or rather old past patterns and actions needing to be released once and for all; preferably in this lifetime. Coming out of our attachments to desires and the positive or negative affect of experiences but staying in a neutral state of being always aware of our connection as the Divine (Atma) Itself is what gets us out of the cycle of karma and death and rebirth. This process can be smooth for most of us. As we listen to our hearts, our Angels, and the Divine, we flow through life awake, aware, joyful, and blissful.

Honor <u>your</u> process. After all, it is only your path and nobody else's. Have patience with yourself as well. Sometimes things won't happen as fast as you, or rather your ego, would like. But know that it is all Divine and everything happens as it should. Your path is yours alone. You may have spikes of activity and bliss and other days, weeks or months are seemingly lifeless. But they are not lifeless. They are filled with life lessons and challenges that you may need to face in order to continue your process. Sometimes your awakening will be active with physical symptoms and other times you are only processing emotional issues. It is unique to everyone. Honor YOUR path. See it as Divine and stay in that positive mindset that all is truly in Divine order.

It is amazing to see the transformations occurring within all of humanity. It is all divine and occurring in a timing that is just right for each of us. There is no need to rush or push yourself or anyone else. We will all get there in the time that is right for us. Simply follow your heart. We are naturally progressing into a new human race; blossoming like flowers.

My Journey

If you're reading this book you may want to hear a teeny bit about me and my story to show you where I am coming from. Here I will share briefly a bit about me. Included in the second book, *Divine Embrace*, is a more detailed account of my awakening experiences. Today, I am an Energy Worker as well as a Yoga and Spiritual Teacher. With the energy healing that I offer, I regard myself as simply the channel by which the Divine flows through to the person coming for a session.

During my previous transformational years, from the very first Kundalini energy awakening I felt back in 2000, I have transformed into a new being. Powerful changes to the core have occurred within my physical, mental, emotional and spiritual well-being. Changes in me and my life that I made on many levels occurred. I continue to blossom more fully into the divine being I am and always have been.

Back in 2000, I asked for a divorce from my, then, Husband. I shed 90 pounds after ten years of ups and downs with weight by eating better, working out and the key ingredient to shedding and keeping the weight off was connecting to my Divine Spiritual Self. In combination with this connection to Spirit I utilized feeling, being and envisioning my thinner physical body using the Law of Attraction, Energy (like Reiki), as well as surrendering and allowing. I also released a lifetime of poor relationship patterns as well as other unconscious patterns. Many other patterns and blockages continue to be released and still do. My "Shadow" comes out and teaches me the lessons I am to learn. The process of moving through the "Shadow challenges" that occur rip away the layers to shine forth my true self.

Prior to my awakening I was simply going through life with total unconsciousness. And since then, I am a new person. Back then, I was living unconsciously, fighting with life and its circumstance and felt deprived of passion and purpose. I kept to myself most of my growing up years. Not speaking most times so that I wouldn't look silly or be belittled by someone. Hiding in a corner reading books at family visits or events. I even fell asleep at a heavy metal concert! :) (But I blame that on the uncanny ability to be able to sleep anywhere if I want to, teehee.) And back then I simply just did not have the desire to extend out much. I was so unconscious that I didn't realize that it didn't and does not have to be this way. My ego and the mass consciousness out there ruled me rather than my Divine soul.

Now my personality is more open, loving and free. There is still, of course, more work to be done. But I've grown into a person that I actually like now. My self-esteem is now high on the Richter scale. I am active with physical fitness (total opposite to my lazy growing up years). I am involved deeply with yoga now and am Certified Vinyasa Yoga Teacher. Yoga helps me move through life. Yoga is living life in the flow. Meditation is a daily ritual for me that brings such peace and stillness to my life. I can draw on this anytime and anywhere for peace. Although I was intrigued with spirituality beforehand, it is at a much higher volume now. My spiritual studies are in-depth, whereas before I only read fiction. Much of these studies include Reiki, Integrated Energy Therapy, Magnified Healing and many other energy healing modalities, as well as clearing methods such as Ho'oponopono, Huna and Peace Messenger for the Land and Body. All of which I have integrated into my being and created a unique sacred energy awakening process that I share with you in the second book, *Divine Embrace*.

I experience wonderful states of bliss, expanded consciousness, stillness, love, devotion to the Divine, and gratitude for my life and family. Much of my time is also in the here and now, experiencing and living life! I channel Divine energy as an energy healer. Energy is a gift and I am so blessed to share it! A life of service to the Divine and assisting others in their awakening has evolved as a part of my Divine path. A life of service is something that is inherent within most all of us and it is also the way of the Tao. Spiritual insights and creative writing flow through me. Divine intuition is a strong guiding force for me now. It pulls me in the direction I am meant to go. I've written this book! Because I am more naturally in tune with the Divine, manifesting comes much easier. As you are in tune with the Divine, your desires match that of your Divine path and naturally things will occur to meet you in that space. You are always fully supported by the Universe. The flow of life is smoother for me now more so than before. My conviction and belief of the Divine is my constant driving force. Life feels more meaningful and fulfilling than ever before.

There's so much more that I am healing and working through every day. It is amazing and continues in my own natural way that works for my soul. A transformation that is now speeding up and I am riding the waves of bliss as they come! This energy is a catalyst for positive change in every aspect of our lives. I face challenges knowing my present moment is always my savior as it connects me to the Divine and nothing compares to that connection.

These spiritual experiences we are faced with every day transforms or, rather, allows us to finally remember the divine beings we already are. It may take a lifetime or can happen in an instant. I am a new person from my experiences and I continue to evolve. I know in my soul that this is a blossoming we will all process, transform and reach in our own natural time and in our own natural way. It is all Divine.

Do It Anyway

People are often unreasonable, irrational, and self-centered.
Forgive them anyway.

If you are kind, people may accuse you of selfish, ulterior motives.
Be kind anyway.

If you are successful, you will win some unfaithful friends and some genuine enemies.
Succeed anyway.

If you are honest and sincere people may deceive you.
Be honest and sincere anyway.

What you spend years creating, others could destroy overnight.
Create anyway.

If you find serenity and happiness, some may be jealous.
Be happy anyway.

The good you do today, will often be forgotten.
Do good anyway.

Give the best you have, and it will never be enough.
Give your best anyway.

In the final analysis, it is between you and God.
It was never between you and them anyway.

~ Version is credited to Mother Teresa

Part I

Natural Universal Laws

Chapter 1

Our Divine Angel Helpers

Angels have been very prominent in my life. When I require peace of mind, they are there. When I require guidance they are there. When I am feeling low they are there. And when I am feeling uplifted they are there! Angels are higher vibrational frequency beings that are pure and here to assist us in our evolvement. They are our loving guides. They are the soft whispers you hear so often.

When you ask with intention, they are there! So ask and you will receive their guidance in an instant! Have trust and this will put you in a place of allowing the communication to happen more easily. Intend, communicate your request and listen to EVERY whisper and intuition you receive. Remember, something seemingly small could be the one thing that ties together a request you have made.

Some say our Angels communicate with us. Some say it is a Spiritual Guide. Some say their spiritual guides are extraterrestrial as well. Some say it is our twin flame/other half of ourselves. Some have mentioned receiving this guidance from the blue light of consciousness itself. And some say it is our Higher Self. At different times it could be one or the other but I feel the truth is always based in my heart. We are, in the "end", all One. But these "separate" aspects make up the Whole. We work to integrate these parts of ourselves and ascend.

The Angels are assisting us in eradicating negative blocks and energies. And they are assisting us in ascension. Whether we are consciously aware of them or not, they are helping. As you become more conscious of the Angels assistance you may notice a more powerful and smooth transformation process occurring. The Angels assist us with our questions, confusion and symptoms that may occur in our body as we awaken. Their guidance can clear the way; Guidance like listening to their yearnings and assistance for a clear body free of toxins, and listening to such guidance for our physical bodies and for our planet as a whole. The Angels guide us away from polluting the planet and our bodies.

The Angels send us the message that our thoughts are powerful. Thoughts truly are things and they want us to clean up our thoughts. As we train ourselves and recondition our brains and soul to know how beautiful we are and how much we deserve all good things in life, the more we attract good things. However, the more you think negatively, the more negative experiences you will attract and thereby making your ascension process much more difficult. The Angels are teaching us the Universe Laws such as the Law of Attraction and the Law of Allowing (more on these laws to follow in the next few chapters). The Angels bring with them the Power of affirmations, meditations, positive thinking, energy connections, natural living guidance, love, and so much more.

We are all evolving into multidimensional beings. We are Angels in training. I found this message from the Angels so profound! The Angels sent me the new wisdom that we are all Angels and those of us here on Earth are simply emerging into those Angels through our lives here on Earth. When I received

4

this wisdom I then came across a variety of more well-known spiritual teachers that were saying the same thing. This was a strong confirmation sent to me from the Angels that what they shared with me and what I perceived is correct.

There is a hierarchy in the higher realms as well. Each person, Spirit Guide and Angel are at different frequencies. We each have a soul signature; each at a specific sound, color, vibration. How we express ourselves energetically is our unique chord within the body of God. We can all evolve into Angels as our vibrations rise up because we are *all* Angels. Isn't that amazing! We are all Angels and have been prior to incarnating. Some Angels, ArchAngels for instance such as ArchAngel Michael (one of my favorites), choose to stay in the Angelic realm, never to incarnate and assist from there. And we, as Angels, decided to learn through living in contrast in this dimension. There are infinite numbers of dimensions all leading to unity with the Divine. All paths lead to the same. The Angels that chose to stay in the Angelic realm have the agreement that they will assist us as guides and work with us as we request it. It is their joy to do so! We can open up our awareness more and more to go into new dimensions. Although we are all One, the Angelic realm is one of the highest dimensions.

The Angels that have chosen to stay in the Angelic realm are on a slightly different plane (a different dimension or realm), and have their Divine purpose of working with humans. Angels, especially Guardian Angels, (there are many types of Angels) seem to be more the type to hover nearby and assist in emergencies even without our asking them to. (But only if it is not in our Soul's purpose to go through whatever emergency may be happening. Highest and best, good always.)

Angels, unless it's an emergency, **must** be asked for their help in your life. Free will is human law. The Angels respect this law. So they cannot help without our asking. Ask and they are more than willing and even waiting for you to simply ask so they can help you (for your highest and best good of course!) Angels know no limits. They are boundless but will not get involved in your life without you first giving them your permission by asking. They love to help us, but require us to ask for what we desire so they can assist. They cannot act beyond what is in our blueprints (contracts for life). The Angels have a higher awareness of the All and know where they can and cannot assist depending upon our life lessons we decided to go through once we incarnate.

The Angels that I connect with bring such heart and love emotions. If you ever have doubts that you are talking to your Angels, Guides or Masters in the Spiritual Realm, just simply listen to your heart. Your heart speaks the truth in the depths of your soul.

Taking action allows our paths to align in higher ways. Ascending happens through clearing energy blockages held within ourselves. And the Angels are helping in many ways to assist us with this goal always. They bring tips on meditation, to open the channels, tips on clearing your aura, cutting negative cords attached to you, tips on natural living, and tips for aligning more with our hearts. And what I am sharing with you in this book series will provide such answers and clarity.

It is one of the most important jobs of the Angels to assist us in awakening to our true Divine path in life. Aligning with our true soul's calling creates ripples and awakenings that are a part of ascension. What is our true soul's calling. Well, it seems to be divided into two categories. One is your outer purpose and two is your inner purpose. Everyone's inner purpose is to awaken to the Divine within them. Or if you like, to become the Angels they already are and remembering who they already are! Take a moment in stillness right now as you read this and feel the truth in this. You are Divine and always have been. The distractions out "there" have taken you away from this inner truth. And now you can breathe deeply and know you are a spiritual being having a human experience.

Our external purpose or outer purpose is something that pulls at us individually, a joyful tug into a way of working with the physical reality right now. This tug can take you into a new career or one that remains consistent throughout your life. For some it is getting out there and producing something tangible for the world at-large to see. And for others it is holding the space by living a life of purpose and presence in no matter what they choose as their career or way of life. These people are simply being in the present blissful moment while they go through the mundane tasks of life, but enjoying every minute of it because this is their purpose in this life. Knowing that you are in your bliss is enough to know you are following the right path for YOU. No one else can tell you what that is. Only you can. Your compass is your bliss. Follow your bliss. It's your spiritual compass. I speak more in-depth about living your destiny of purpose in chapter 29.

The Angels are always guiding us to our purpose. This agreement with them is preplanned as they are joyfully our guides. As they assist, we align and feel more love, more in tune and closer to the connection that's always been there. The Divine. Call on your Angels. Listen. Take Action. Awaken.

Chapter 2

Laws of Attraction, Allowing & Free Will

> "The basis of most physical human confusion, is this. Everything is about the Law of Attraction. Which means, everything is about 'inclusion.' There is no such thing as 'exclusion' . . . You can't look at something and say no, no, I want that NOT . . . and have it go away, because your attention to it, causes you to vibrate WITH IT and by law of attraction, it then comes to you." ~ Abraham-Hicks

What we see in our world and in ourselves is a reflection of what we ourselves are putting out to the Universe. We **are** 100% responsible for everything we see, hear, feel and create in our lives. Sit up, take notice and take action. If you quietly go back into "slumber land" (unconsciousness) you will miss out on so much and the result is catastrophic, because whether you are aware or unaware of the fact that we create our reality ourselves, you will STILL create that reality. Our vibration created the reality we live in right now. For most of us, it seems we must first wake up to the true nature of reality; become conscious; live consciously. Then we can dive deeper to our true essence that is always there, always watching. At least this is how it is working for me; a natural progression to our true Self.

Your beliefs and memories start you out in your subconscious. From there you have your thoughts. Words hold consciousness and a vibration all their own. These words aka your thoughts take form into Emotions. Emotion charges. Emotions equal energy. Energy emits out to the Universe and like the magic you just spun you've received back a situation, circumstance or experience from your very own thoughts/ beliefs/emotions/vibrational energy. This is the **Law of Attraction**. We truly **are** the genies in our own life. I've had too many experiences that tell me that this is Universal Law.

Combine the Law of Attraction with the Law of Allowing and the flow of receiving what you desire is imminent. The **Law of Allowing** is the simple act of trusting in the Divine and surrendering to the outcome of the highest and best, good of all concerned. The simple act of surrender alone is freeing. Of course the goal here (I assume for many) is to feel good, at peace and free. So we want to feel those good emotions NOW, not later or when this happens or that happens, but RIGHT NOW. Feeling it now attracts MORE of that to you! :)

You must let go of whatever it is you are trying to manifest. In order to receive it, you must give it off to the Universe to take care of it. In order to really detach from this, see it as if you have already received it! Because you HAVE! Let it go. Surrender. KNOW you already HAVE IT! Believe. Let it go! Have FAITH! Then it is yours! The Law of Allowing at its best.

The key here is to have nonattachment to all desires. If you are divinely guided to pursue something then you can place that vibration out there. But you must remember that you are always supported. When you act only in selfless service for the Divine in everything that you do, then you are supported always. Everything always works out. That doesn't mean sit back on your couch and watch. That means flow with life. Live Divinely. Act out of selfless service in every mundane thing you do and give it all up to the Divine. Every morsel. I am not talking about giving away everything you own. I am talking about surrendering your attachment to it all whether it's there or not there. It matters not. Feel the deep true Self (God self) within and only devote yourself to That. Follow divine guidance, such as signs, synchronicities, or a pull to act and act with selfless service. You can live a life of peace only when you surrender the desire for it. It seems for me, that I was able to come to this knowing (and still working with it) by first working with creation and utilizing the law of attraction. Now I am slowly realizing that I can create or I can simply give it up. When I create from desire and attachment suffering ensues because I am within the world of polarity. But if I see that everything I am pulled to say, be or act is a selfless service to the Divine then I am always taken care of. Things always work out but mostly I am in my inner peace. Challenges will occur but I will be in my True Self knowing it is all Divine. When you are in this place all things that you need are provided for you with ease. You are always taken care of. It is not about positive or negative. It's about consciousness.

As a stepping stone to the surrendering act and connecting to your True Divine Self, it takes dedication, a positive outlook, and forgiveness of self and others. One thing that helped me, that I strongly suggest you do, is create a *Gratitude Journal*. Right down ALL the good in your life. And I mean ALL the good. If you need to first get out all the bad, write it down, process it, then BURN that journal/paper (this is very good for releasing all the bad once and for all and you're telling God you're not going to accept that ickiness in your life anymore). Then EVERY DAY write down at least three things you are grateful for. (At least!) I know when I got started, I couldn't stop at three. Do this for 21 days or more! After the 21 days, if you ever get in a funk do this exercise again. It works to adjust your brain waves to expecting more positive things to be grateful for. It also brings peace. I sometimes read over my gratitude journal and get uplifted simply by hearing what I have been grateful for.

The best most potent ways to raise your vibration and attract that which you desire of a constant state of peace and bliss is to consciously choose where to focus your attention. This is the **Law of Free Will**. Aim your focus on positive experiences. Choose to see the many encouraging people in the world, and the beauty in every moment, and in nature. Surround yourself with seeing every sparkle of happiness, beauty and love that surrounds every moment. Even the not-so-great moments hold beauty, peace and bliss. Each moment is a gift. Ask what this moment offers you as its gift now. See the Divine even in the things that are not positive, because they are there. God is in everything, everyone and every place you see. The wise person is someone who can see the Divine in everything. The wise person is the person who can see the Divine even during times of suffering. Doing even only this is powerful and can shift your consciousness to higher more pure vibration permanently.

Be conscious of EVERY moment you are alive. I feel that with all of the areas of our lives in balance (i.e. relationships, work, play, mental, emotional, spiritual and physical), knowing you attract all you desire in your life and making a conscious effort for it to be positive, a beautiful life experience follows. Although life will happen, there is a more peaceful flow. So knowing you attract all you think on and FEEL, remember this and do NOT dwell or focus on the negative. Do not bury your negative emotions, but rather recognize them for their positive assistance in contrast. Allow yourself to be in the space with them and then healthily release them (by either breathing, movement, meditation or any number of releasing methods). Remember, what you need to do is be true to YOU in every moment. So if you're feeling a certain way you must let those emotions out in the healthiest way, so that they RELEASE and then they don't clutter your mind and body and you can move faster into happier states of being. It's the healthy way. By accepting the negative aspects of yourself, recognizing them, taking the lessons needed and then releasing them, you are accepting that polar opposite you. You are becoming balanced within your entire being. You are telling your higher self you are ready for the next level of Ascension.

Now, on to the positive side of things. Living in memories of the bad or "negative" will only keep you in that energy and bring more experiences of that same vibration/feeling. No more wallowing. So even when it's hard (and believe me I KNOW) think positive. See the divine lessons in the suffering you incurred and live Divine from that experience. Think of a funny moment that makes you laugh. Smile at yourself in the mirror even when you don't want to. Think of a baby you love, anything HAPPY or loving and you start to vibrate at that level/ feeling and you will receive more experiences of that HAPPY feeling. It will pick up in momentum the more you do this and the more you raise your vibration to the higher more loving, happier feelings and experiences.

All of this starts to lift you out of that funk. By lifting your vibration you will also then NO MORE attract the "icky" stuff in your life. No more accidents, no more negative people, no more feeling bad, no more physical issues. Do note that the "icky" people will just naturally flow out of your life too. You no longer need those people and more positive wonderful people that match your vibration will come to you naturally! Now, that doesn't take out Divine lessons or challenges you set in stone for your life, so remember that when things happen. Things will happen, and it's how YOU decide to react to it, that gets you attracting what comes next. Choose positive happy loving energy, even when you don't want to. Especially when you don't want to. Again, I can't say it enough, see the divine lessons in what you experience but attach nothing to it, not desire, not anger, nothing. Simply connect with your True Self within and know that everything is perfect.

An excellent practice to do is to remember what positive aspects of yourself make you and other people happy. Are you funny, outgoing and loving? Do you take on an extra task so that someone else doesn't have to do too much sometimes? Do you share a special talent that you love and make others happier because of it? Natural processing aside, you can shift your consciousness to a more elevated way of feeling and being in seconds. It's the flip of a switch.

The strongest way to manifest is through stimulating all the senses, using thought, word, deed and action. Combining all of these actions is powerful. It is all intention-based. You will come to a space where simply your intention will manifest and until that time comes and even when it does you may still use the stimulation of all your senses to gain a greater result. There is something to be honored with ritual and ceremonies. Remember, keep that connection to Source, act only with selfless service, surrender everything and detach from the outcome.

So we first think and feel our desires. Then we vocalize our desires in a positive manner. A step that is also the power of sound and this embeds into our subconscious. Writing down our desires is the next step that, also, infuses this into our brains and subconscious. We may even also create a vision board for this step. (A vision board is simply visuals of desires you would like to receive. For example, magazine cut-outs pasted on a piece of paper you have designated as your vision board for manifesting.) After this we surrender and let it go to the Universe. Finally we take action. Something will come to us by way of intuition or offerings from our surrounding (people or our environment). I like to call it Divine intuition. We then jump at the chance to follow-through with the plans set in motion from our asking. As you take those action steps that come to you the easier more steps flow to you and the faster your desire manifests.

Giving allows you to receive. Giving is a great way to be in the moment of abundance now. As we give selflessly with no need or want to receive anything in return we are there in that moment able to receive that which we give multiplied. And so from giving, you find oneness and from that connection arises your destiny and the circle happens. So in the very moment you are in the state of being that which you desire, you are giving yourself the energy state of receiving it. If you are already in a rich wealthy state of mind, you will receive it. It is only by feeling it as if it's already there that it comes to you. That is why it's easier for the rich to become richer with money, as they already have it! So they are acting in what they already have.

So BE as if you already are wealthy, healthy, happy, and peaceful. Try each one for moments a day. Be in every moment as if this is the only moment you have, because it truly is the only moment you have! Be present! Life comes alive! Then you will most easily be in the flow. You will easily give to others around you with simple gestures as a smile, allowing another to go first and even bigger gestures. It all flows in a nice circle connecting us all together divinely.

Oneness is our divine connection to the Source. We ARE the Divine and the Divine IS US! The more I feel this connection the louder this truth is felt within me. We are connected to everyone and every thing! As we are connected and feel that divine connection we then feel the inner tingles of our Destiny! Our passions, our desires are our destiny. The divine flows through us, the expression, our passions (our dance) in life needs to be expressed! As you follow your true path abundance in all things flows to you naturally.

When you master the art of connecting to the Divine while utilizing the Law of Attraction, Allowing and Free Will you align yourself with the Universe and the Universe with you. Magic occurs!

Law of Free Will

Now, let's look a little deeper at the Law of Free Will. The Law of Free Will is that you choose your path. In every moment you are choosing something. We do this unconsciously a lot of the times. However, the more you practice and fine tune listening to yourself, your thoughts, your emotions, the more you will make more conscious choices that better serve YOU! Your divine self.

We choose to allow the ripple that comes our way to affect us and also pass on the ripple effect. We receive negative or positive ripples and some variation in between. We need to become more conscious of what ripples are coming our way. If it does not serve you and your divine self anymore, then

CHOOSE to rid yourself of it. Transmute those undesired energies into positive. We have the choice to take on those more negative ripples or energies that come our way and pass them on to others. We CHOOSE to pass them on. The more you become conscious of a negative experience that may come your way, the more you can stop it in its tracks and put the blocks up, feel what you need to feel and send pure love, light and transmutation to this energy.

We are all connected. We are energy beings and even when we think we are alone, we are not truly. So what we feel does move forward through the currents and emanates out to those we are feeling or thinking about. We also must remember that we attract the next experience into our lives by what we are feeling right now. We've attracted everything. Each person and experience is a mirror for what is inside of us. Even if that person or experience is negative, thank the person and experience for mirroring what you are putting out with your energy to show you what you may want to change and if the experience feels good, what you may want to keep flowing to you.

If the experience is negative, you do not need to send it on to the next person in your path (your kids, your family, friends or co-workers or even the vendors you come across in your daily life). You can choose to put on that smile and FEEL HAPPY and LOVED right NOW and pass THAT on. By doing this, flipping that switch, you changed the spiral of energy. You created a positive current that will flow along to the next person who can choose to take that uplifting energy or not. Choosing what feels right, good and true is our free will. What do you choose? It's your Free Will.

DECIDE you can do it! You are capable of so much more thank you think. You can do it! This truth is BURSTING from within me to scream at the world as it is being screamed from within me! We get what we expect. And you will see the results you expect. Decide you will see what you are desiring, really put yourself in that frame of BEING and you WILL. I feel the energy build in its intensity whenever I remember that I can

DECIDE to see what I am desiring! Suddenly it IS there! It's amazing how fast this can work!!!

I feel it in my workouts. I wake up in the morning and am not always gung-ho for a rigorous cardio routine. And just today as my warm-up commenced I got into the feeling state of being ready to go all out. I decided right then and there that my energy was HIGH and I had plenty to really give it my all and enjoy it at the same time. I felt my energy immediately build up and move my body almost effortlessly. Each punch, kick and jab had beautiful energy backing it for more powerful results. Each compilation of moves drove me further as I enjoyed the variety of the workout. The music in my workouts so divinely timed assisted me in really getting into it even more. I took every kick and jump higher and loved it! The workout was over before I knew it. Chalene Johnson of *Turbo Fire* knows this secret and shares her wisdom of free will during the *Turbo Fire* workouts I love. As she reminds you that you can pick up your energy right now simply by deciding you can do it, you suddenly gain a boost of energy and enjoy the last minutes of the workout that is left. It's amazing what we can do when we decide we can!

Just decide you've got it and you DO! What's great is there really doesn't have to be much physical effort. You just simply move into the state of being that is already there and boom it's there. You are aligned. It's that quick. You build that energy from within and move out any negative thoughts that are holding you back. They aren't real, just an illusion. Just swipe them away. They no longer exist in your reality. Something better has taken its place and you simply uplift you vibration with that decision.

As the amazing and uplifting Life Coach, Anthony Robbins says, "Beliefs have the power to create and the power to destroy. Human beings have the awesome ability to take any experience of their lives and create a meaning that dis-empowers them or one that can literally save their lives."

You allow your vibration to move into the higher vibration of consciousness that's always been there. Your true Divine self emerges. Choose the magical, happy, fulfilling, uplifting life you were always meant to live. Discard all the rest. Discard the past, discard old past patterns of negativity, hate, jealousy, greed, and unconsciousness. Embrace the true divine nature within you. The real you that is open, loving, truthful, happy, joy-filled and uplifted into the magic of All That Is. It is your true essence after all. Decide you are in alignment with the true self that is you and you ARE. Shift your consciousness and you are there in an instant. You can do it. You are doing it. It's an act of surrender to a better way. A way that is innate within us all. It is natural. And it is your Free Will.

Chapter 3

Thought Equals Outcome

W hen talking about the Law of Attraction, Allowing and Free Will, the next natural step is being mindful of our thoughts and how they tie in tremendously with our vibration and the results we expect from our intentions. The key still comes back to being consciously aware. Our thoughts become thought forms. These thought forms create more of whatever they hold. So if they are holding negative energy because of negative thoughts, they will create more negative energy. However, if they hold positive energy because of positive happy or loving thoughts they will create more positive energy. It is obvious here that the goal is to feel more positive and blissful. The goal to reach full self-realization is becoming neutral to all situations by seeing all situations as gifts or rather not good or bad. In order to reach this state one must become very present with their thoughts. Our thoughts create our emotions and vice versa. These thoughts go out into the Universe and also the person you may be aiming them at or near.

"All that we are is the result of what we have thought."
~ Buddha

If you are consciously aware of your state of being at all times you are more likely to be above others' thought forms and their attachments. You will be in a better state of mind and vibration. So that energy will pass you by. You will be blissfully transparent. However, if you are in an unconscious state of mind you are more susceptible to the influence of thought energy.

Speak to others from your heart. A wonderful idea I heard about recently was to speak to someone as if it's from your heart, not your mind. See your words and love flow through your heart to the people you come in contact with. Feel that love flow to them. Thanking them silently for their presence in your life.

I do feel vibration is the key to remember. Sound vibration gets us there, feeling (emotions) gets us there, Love and happiness are the ultimate vibrations that release us from the "ties that bind". If we can keep those vibrations up and alive within us as often as possible, then our vibrations are at their peek to not only receive all things good (including the blissful state of this Love and happiness vibration) but also to spread it to others! In sharing our love with others we raise our vibrations as well as others vibrations. As we are in our highest of vibrations, just our mere presence in this state causes a shift in the positive direction.

Also, important to keep in mind is that vibrations are in everything. Everything is energy and vibration. The ocean holds its own very high vibration. Just going to the ocean, seeing the waves crashing and hearing the ocean waves uplifts your soul. Just as being in the vortices of Sedona, Arizona will do the same. The higher vibrations of this spot on the planet emanate through you and raise your vibrations. The stones at Stonehenge also hold a higher vibration. You get the gist.

There are some things that hold a vibration just in the visual, some in the sound and the combination of the vibration within seeing and hearing bring about the vibrational emotion/feeling as well! These combinations all contribute to your vibration. It is your choice whether you expose yourself to higher or lower vibrations. And for me, I have been on a spiral upward in choosing higher vibrations. Choose what feels good to you! Our emotions are our internal guidance system! Ask yourself in every moment: "Does this truly make me feel good?" If so, then you are on the right track! Follow your bliss.

One method for squashing those unwanted or negative thought forms is to visualize them going. You can visualize them as what you think they might look like and then send pure divine light energy to them or a rainbow of colored energy to them that transmutes these thoughts forms into pure divine energy. My favorite visualization brings in the Violet Flame of St. Germain. You can call on the Violet Flame of St. Germain and again visualize the purple flame transmuting these thoughts into pure divine beautiful energy, cleaning you, your aura and the air around you. If you've sent these thoughts to another visualize the same in the other person. Ask for only pure divine loving energy to be sent their way and cleanse them of any impurities you unconsciously sent their way. Ask for it to be transmuted and so it will be.

You can shift your presence to a feeling of love for yourself and for others. In this conscious shift you raise your vibrations keeping you in higher states of being. You can call on ArchAngel Michael to come forth and use his golden sword to sever all negative cords and attachments from you to others that are of negative affect and ask that only positive, love and light remain. This is very powerful. You can do it very quickly or take a few minutes to see the Angel at work. Turn on music that lifts your spirits. Music is very powerful. It can change your mood so fast and thus your vibration. That is why it is wise to remain conscious of what music you are listening to and when. Keep it to the mood you truly want to be in or you might get caught in an unconscious whirlwind of a vibrational shift you didn't count on. Sometimes it's a nice surprise and others times it is not what you counted on! If you become conscious of the music not being what you desire, change it to something uplifting. And lastly, don't forget to do an aura and chakra cleansing daily, as this will clear your field daily to start fresh. (I have included one cleansing option in Book Two *Divine Embrace* and the *Divine Embrace Meditation CD* is available on my website, www.SpiritualCompassConnection. com, for this purpose as well.)

The outcome of anything observed is going to take on the results/expectations of the observer; as research results suggest. Such research can be found in the awesome movie: "What the Bleep do we Know!?" I've witnessed this myself with my life experiences and working with the Law of Attraction. Just by merely observing an experiment we change the outcome with our very own energies/thoughts/ vibrations/expectations.

In the end, however, I feel we are all one and are all contributing to the collective consciousness and making our impact on the world in this way. I say, let's use our powers for good and feel, expect and be in our state of love & bliss and affect the consciousness in a positive way.

Use your intuition. It knows deep within what feels right to you. We each vary in the way that works best for us. We each have our way that works in perfect divine order. Where the Yoga path might work for one, the Tao way will work for another. All paths lead to the same. Feel your way. It's in your bliss where you find your truth.

New Version of You

I absolutely love the old theme song *New Version of You* from the, now cancelled, show called Felicity. *New version of you* is a song challenging you to find a new version of yourself and be who you truly are within. Felicity was a college student who, moved by something a boy named Ben wrote in her yearbook, changed her college choice and followed Ben across country from California to a college in NY after graduating high school. In return for her behavior she ended up first finding out more about herself rather than a boy she felt compelled to get to know better.

Sometimes signs and synchronicities will come to you through books, television, people and many other avenues. The messages come to you when you need to hear it most. Peak up and listen. Today while finishing up getting ready for work, I turned on the TV for a minute and a rerun of Coach was on. Coach was telling Luther that he was too negative. He had inadvertently, through his own fear of flying, caused their entire football team to miss a game because he refused to fly, forcing the entire team to ride the train. This train ended up getting stuck behind a cow, and then further a snow storm stopped them in their tracks. Coach told Luther he needed to change. Luther said, "Okay. Done. I'm changed." Coach told him that it's not that easy. He further passionately stated that Luther needed to change his entire lifestyle, his way of living, his way of thinking, his entire way of being, to rid himself of all the negativity he was sinking further into. Luther had been causing a chain reaction of negativity affecting all those around him. A helicopter ended up coming during that precious life-changing moment and Luther said he would start right now and be the first to be rescued into the helicopter. We see Luther succeed in crushing his fears and rising above his current negative situation literally & symbolically, by making a change for the positive in this gesture. He could have easily stayed in the train till ground crews came in two days . . . but he rose above. We see this as a visual when he is raised up by the Helicopter. That's a strong message!

The more positive we are, the higher our vibration becomes and it seems easier to connect with our peaceful center; our connection to the Divine; our True Self. The higher our vibration is the less negative situations, people, and thoughts affect our being. The less negativity is attracted to us and the less we put out to the Universe that negativity is something we want to attract. There will probably be negativity around and challenges yet to face; however, you will know NOT to focus on it or attach yourself to it as you progress. It is not the main focus point. Neither is the positive. What is the main focus point is consciousness, the deep inner Self.

You will know that even those negative people can't affect YOU unless you **allow** them to. You will be able to see the lessons these seemingly negative people provide you. They are your mirrors and your angels. You can shoot those "negative" people a beam of white light, knowing we are all connected. I love to allow my inner self to see them as they truly are at the core of their being. I will say in my mind: "I acknowledge and honor you as a light being." And then the light being they are comes to me and I feel amazing as I hope they do as well. Disconnect from their actions, don't judge and just know that they are dealing with issues within the level they are in at that very moment in time; just as you are. Don't let their negative actions affect your future actions in that negative way. Energy comes in waves. You can **choose** to let their negativity pass you by or you can choose to keep that wave of negativity going. You can see the effect you have on yourself and others when you choose to keep the negativity going. It affects pretty much your whole day (or worse) and spirals out of control affecting all those around you. Vice versa, you can see how good it feels to just let it pass you by. Even surround them with white light, give them a little positive gesture if you can or at least a positive thought. By letting it go and staying in the positive energies, you will then see a chain reaction of positive events take place instead. How wonderful it is to keep yourself in that mode!

Now, I am not discounting certain situations where righteous action is needed. Those situations where the Universe has put someone in your path that you need to stand your ground with. In some cases you are to teach them something, as they teach you; even if it's only on the subliminal energy transference levels. In those situations, you do still need to be aware of going into the "negative" zone. Say your peace in all the positivity that you can muster. With time it gets easier. Suddenly, you'll notice more and more that you are out of your ego mind and are able to say the words of the Zen master (told by Eckhart Tolle in his book *A New Earth*), "Is that so?" to whatever situation you run into. And in this passive state you are not uncaring, you are just NOT playing the drama role anymore. You are OUT of the game and are not manifesting that negative energy. You are within your true divine self. Stick to your goals in having the highest and best, good for all as the outcome. See only positive solutions occurring and you attract that positive solution to you.

I choose waves of positive energy rather than the opposite. Start a new wave today. See something wonderful and smile, smile to another or pay someone a compliment, help others where you can, feel the positive energy wave flow out to others and by seeing others sore, you rise up.

I've noticed and keep hearing that we are all ascending now. Many people are waking up to realize they have been living in a dream and going along with what others have said was what "to do". Now you and others realize that we aren't living the life WE truly desire within and can NOW make changes to do just that. We deserve to live our passions and be happy, so the time is now. :)

Negativity can stop you in your tracks, if you let it. It's a pile of quick sand that if you don't rise above, you could sink to the bottom. Someone recently told me that the only way to get out of quicksand was to lift your feet up out of the quick sand in order to float. I challenge you to see that **new version of you**, lift your feet up and rise above those negative thoughts, actions, situations and people!

Unconditioning

Now, let's move into the idea of removing the patterns that bind our thoughts into stagnant negativity. Have you ever had one of those days where you swear you did everything the same as your usual daily routine, only for something to shift and make you say "I could have sworn . . ." On such a day, prior to starting off on my regular walk in the middle of my workday, I had a mini-crisis. I couldn't find my cell phone.

I looked high and low in my cubicle at work, in my purse and bag. Checked, double-checked and re-checked. My routine has been that my cell phone stays in my purse until I walk up the three flights of stairs to my cubicle at work. From there I proceed to take my cell phone out of my purse and take my purse downstairs to the cafeteria, buy whatever I may want to buy, grab my two waters and head back upstairs and start working. It's been my routine for as long as I have worked in this corporation (years).

On this day, something shifted. When I got in to work a small group of co-workers gathered early, so I put my stuff down quickly and followed them down with my trusty purse in hand, did my normal routine of getting a piece of candy (usually a tootsie roll or something: my one cheat during work hours—notice I said during work hours! haha!) and my two waters and walked back upstairs with my co-workers.

At around 11a.m., the time I tend to do my first walk of the day, I got my badge and reached in my trusty drawer for my trusty cell phone and it wasn't there. Huh? As you know, I searched and searched. I told my co-worker, who saw me frantically on my knees searching drawers and bags that I could have sworn I took it out of my purse prior to walking downstairs with them to the cafeteria. It was hardly to be questioned, as this was my routine. I decided to go on my walk without my cell phone and asked the Universe to present it back to me by the time I got back from my walk. I walked down the stairs and just before I opened the door to step outside to another beautiful day, I remembered the first shift in my day.

On this morning I had my cell phone in my purse, as usual, but for some reason got a feeling that I should take it out of my purse and put it in my cup holder because someone might call and I would hear it better (since I like my music a bit loud sometimes). This was odd because I never receive calls that early in the morning. Maybe a rare call from my sister and that's about it. So I did as I had felt pulled to do and put it in my cup holder.

I remembered that my phone was safe and sound and in my car. However, I was not about to run back upstairs and get my car keys to make sure and to also have the phone with me on my walk. So I decided I would do that on my way back in to the office.

From there I had to wonder what the significance of this particular incident meant and I remembered my thoughts from my walk just the day before. I was walking on the beautiful secluded paths outside of my office building with my trusty cell phone in hand and thinking about something I had said to someone about carrying my cell phone on my walks. I had said that I carry it with me "just in case". A-ha! Right there! Just in case? What's that MEAN!? Just in case! I realized that this very thought was going against everything I believe.

I feel that we put thoughts and energies out to the Universe and receive back what we think, feel, desire and feel we deserve to receive. It's been a challenge to UNthink a lot of conditioned beliefs and (surprisingly) thoughts that have been so subtly planted in our brains that these thoughts have become common things we just "say" in passing, that actually deter us from receiving our positive abundance.

I have been going through the process of UNconditioning these types of negative thoughts and connotations for some time now. I watch what I say and think and send more positive energy to counteract anything I realize was one of these conditioned thoughts.

This saying is something I have realized I have been saying "in passing" for some time now and is completely socially accepted as okay to say. The implications of just saying this phrase, "Just in case" doesn't imply good events, although it leaves open a number of possibilities, none are positive. It only holds negative connotations. Just in case what exactly? I refuse to even suggest any examples. We do NOT want our minds going there!

This epiphany went through my head the day before and I just passed them off, continued on my way with my walk. Now today the Universe has intervened to tell me I was on the right track with my train of thought. This course of events I now know happened for a reason. So that I would realize that this "Just in case" is another thought process to UNcondition now. I don't need my cell phone on my walks for "just in case"; maybe if I want to make a call, or check my messages, but not for any other reason.

Have you ever noticed repeating something to your child or someone you know that was said to you when you were a child? These phrases only making sense to you because they were said to you, but when you think about them, they leave you and your child with negative connotation. You do not want to pass on to your children or anyone for that matter, any negative old past patterns that were passed on to you, no matter how socially acceptable it is.

I am continuously becoming more and more aware of these seemingly minor, but huge subliminal messages we send ourselves and releasing them. I realized this particular phrase and need to start practicing taking action with my beliefs with more vigor. This phrase only goes to show that I still have work to do but that's why we're all here!

So I am going forth with practicing what I preach—taking action—talking the talk, walking the walk, thinking the positive thoughts. Are there anymore cliché's I can come up with for this one? ;) I must not only be conscious of what's coming in to my consciousness, but also what is coming out. So I may have stopped watching the news, or exposing myself to negative movies, etcetera, but I still have to recognize that there are conditioned thoughts and phrases that require my conscious **UN**conditioning and actions in order to release them once and for all.

These conditioned thoughts need not hinder us anymore. Realize them and counteract them with a positive thought and/ or action. Eventually they work themselves out of your brain forever! Keep the positive waves going. :)

I went for a second walk today . . . and I didn't take my cell phone.

Chapter 4

Great Expectations

E very day I make it a point to take a break and do some stretches. I find a way to center and bring clarity back to my whole being. When at work, I will usually do this in the bathroom and when the weather is warmer I have a wonderful walking ritual. For the past month now whenever I enter my temporary sanctuary there has been a book there called "Great Expectations". I never read this book. However, I know the name speaks for itself. It has been a wonderful reminder to me of looking to the best of my expectations.

Let's align with our greatest expectations and be in the expecting state of mind as if it's already coming to us or already here! What we expect we get. There is a difference between expecting and being in alignment with our expectations. When something happens that seems unexpected to us on one level, really we are actually in vibrational alignment with that unexpected experience. Something in us is vibrating or resonating with that frequency. So for that surprising experience to happen to you, what you thought you expected is not truly what you are expecting or resonating 100%. The idea here is not to be in that state of needing or wanting it, but rather truly being and feeling that state right now. Letting go of the wanting and needing because if you stay in that feeling state you continuously attract needing and wanting experiences. No matter what, the Universe always always always sends us EXACTLY what we are in vibrational alignment with. Whether you are consciously utilizing the Law of Attraction or not, you *are* using the Law of Attraction. So let's try to consciously shift our whole being.

Let's use financial prosperity as an example, since that is a popular one. We have to remember what we are wanting is not money. Rather, we desire the affects of what money may bring: Peace of mind, bills paid on time, wonderful vacations, and the list goes on. What you can then truly align with and start to feel when stating your desire for financial prosperity is that feeling of Peace, Clarity and Serenity. As you feel this in the NOW, in this very moment you will then be in alignment with that feeling and therefore bring to you experiences that promote Peace, Clarity and Serenity.

Bring yourself to the end result and let your vibration live there! Mike Dooley's *Notes from the Universe* conveys this perfectly, "True, it's not always easy to imagine places you've never been but dream of going, owning things you've never had but dream of having, and being the type of person you've not yet been but have always aspired to be . . . but wouldn't it be easy to imagine the after-party? With best friends and family in the swankiest club you know while your favorite music plays. Proposing toasts, receiving toasts, crying happy tears. Getting hugs, hearing congratulations, leading the conga-line. And otherwise carrying on as you do when you're feeling light as a feather and all the world makes sense."

A conscious effort to change our thoughts, feelings and emotions are the first steps to truly manifesting all you can dream of! Because what we want and desire, wants and desires us! It's our destiny to feel fulfilled, complete, happy and content.

And we share with the world our love of life and living. We are light beings and must honor ourselves as such!

So first we start to work on ourselves. We realize that a lot of our thoughts come from habit and from thoughts and beliefs that were embedded in our cells from childhood and even other lives! This is where we need to be continuously conscious of integrating those opposite polarity patterns. The polarity of negative thinking, the "think the worse so that we are not disappointed when something not-so-great happens" are all on one end of the **polarity pole** I would rather not be on. You can start shifting your polarity to the opposite end, where you expect the best. You think positive thoughts, and then start to actually feel those positive thoughts and as you feel positive, you put positive energy out to the Universe. The Universe hears your call and sees you are resonating at a higher vibrational pattern on that positive polarity pole and starts to bring to you what you are resonating. Those positive experiences! A great book about Polarity is *Divine Magic* by Doreen Virtue. It comes with a CD if you don't have time to read and you can just listen. Amazing!

As you evolve in feeling positive you realize that there are negative experiences. You realize that these experiences do, also, have a valid part in your life. They are valid to aid you in your learning and expanding. As you become more aware of these experiences there is no need to dwell in the negative in order to experience. What you evolve into is actually integrating this "negative" side. As both positive and negative, yin and yang, are valid and need to be integrated. You can accept it, feel it, transmute it into a learning experience where you see the positive experience from it and then healthily release it from your being.

Why I mention this now is because polarity and integration are key instruments for fulfilling your greatest expectations. As you become aware of these sides and shift, you will more consciously be aware of its affect and how to change that frame of mind. So you first become aware of something that flows in, a negative thought or experiences for example. Then you take a step back and observe it rather than react to it. Then you are able to see what lessons it has in store for you, what mirror is this reflecting back to you in order for you to accept and, most important, allow the experience to exist in its perfectness. You can then handle the challenge as you would in a more evolved state of being.

With every challenge there are three options: First, you may feel it is time to let it go and simply be the witness; to observe as I've just discussed. Second, you may feel it is time to face this obstacle head on in beautiful empowerment. Lastly, you may be guided to step aside and leave the situation altogether. Sometimes all of these might be utilized in one situation. Each challenge is unique and divine to each of us.

For instance, in deciding to get divorced to my son's father, several years ago, I went through all of these choices. I tried to change the situation through communication and working through the marriage difficulties. Then I became the witness for a time simply observing. The relationship still felt very dysfunctional and no longer unconditionally loving. So when that didn't feel quite right I moved into taking back my power and dissolving the relationship by asking for a divorce. For me, this was what needed to take place. It felt right and still feels right. For me to raise my vibrations and raise our son healthily and spiritually I had to leave that situation. We are all in a better state of being now. I would not be where I am today had I not taken that divine action from within!

Some lessons may require Divine action (i.e. talking with someone) or may require just sitting and being with the experience. Being the witness. Feel the emotions, let out the anger, sadness or frustrations healthily. And come to a state of forgiveness and allowing. Meditation and exercise are great options for processing. Lastly, you integrate this into your being and release it to the Universe. This process, depending on you and the experience, could take mere minutes, to days, weeks or months. There is no right or wrong.

My husband just told me of a great example from a caller on a recent *Coast to Coast AM Radio Show* who talked about her depression from a falling out with a lover and how to pull yourself out of the mourning process. The host Ian Punnet remarked that its important to note that its okay and healthy to deal with those negative emotions and be in the state for a certain amount of time so as to integrate the experience and to get through it and release it, but you have to decide what's an appropriate length of time to pull yourself out of it. There is a fine line between wallowing and repressing an emotion. So remain conscious of what you are feeling by regularly checking in with yourself.

Remember, the more we resist the experience, the more IN YOUR FACE it will be until you realize you must allow it to be. Allow the experience to exist. Allow the process to flow through you naturally. Surrender! For in doing this, the experience dissipates much faster. Then it's on to more fun in the sun! What's awesome is the more we work with shifting our polarities to the positive side in order to receive our desired results the faster it seems to work. The smoother it seems to feel. Flawlessly we can create faster results as we desire. There are NO LIMITATIONS to what we can do, what we can desire and we can receive and achieve! So think big and let nothing stand in your way because no one really is in your way unless you allow it. Start allowing positive flowing experiences to come your way and receive your greatest expectations now! The time is only now. Enjoy your Greatest Expectations and accept nothing less than the best!

Manifesting

We must manifest from the heart. Manifesting what we truly desire is as simple as **being** what we truly desire. Simple right? We must truly think, feel, act and truly BE what we desire. We put out there to the Universe what we want whether we know it or not. And what we desire must be in line with our heart. We must listen to our heart, not our mind or ego. Our heart and soul knows what is best for us. As we listen to the divine guidance we can take inspired action from this truth from within.

"I don't think I can do it," Luke said.
"Then that is why you fail," said Yoda.

The saying "Use the Force Luke" is one of my favorites. It's almost an internal chant for me. Because in the Star Wars movie Luke learns to use HIS force to create and be more than he ever thought possible. This is also true in LIFE! Just as Yoda taught Luke, we CAN be, if we only believe. We *all* have a force within us. We *all* are part of the Collective/the One that is/God. And we can and do tap into this daily. We can not only help ourselves in consciously manifesting GOOD into our lives, but also the collective consciousness.

When manifesting, you are saying a prayer, casting a spell, thinking positive, or thinking your outcome. It is intention based. Everything is about your intention. As you intend it, it will be so. You not only need to include this portion of manifesting/putting the energy out there, but also taking the physical action to the manifesting. The more you do (in not just putting the energy/request out there) but also in the physical actions you take to meet your goals, the stronger the energy output and the more likely your goal will occur.

Remember we can manifest from our egos or from our Divine self. The more in touch you are with your divine self through methods such as meditation, breathing, just being and following your true bliss, etc., the more you will see the Universe working FOR you. You will see the examples of being in the flow as you allow the Universe to work with you rather than against you. You will be working without doing. Be in the high vibrational energy.

In order to manifest we must train our brains. Our brains usually learn in three different ways. Through:

1. Repetition
2. Trauma
3. Contrast

Repetition makes sense right. Through repetition we always remember what we practicing. Practice makes perfect!

33

So as we repeat a method or process we engrain this into our subconscious and thereby making a shift in the brain to attract at a deeper level. As for Trauma, this is probably the most disliked, but one of the most effective. In any Trauma we are woken up for a dream or rather from unconscious living. We start to be more conscious of what we had been doing from that point and then begin to question everything going forward and change in life altering ways. When we look back we realize that our lives changed for the better due to the traumatic event, even if the event is still painful. It is always a blessing. Lastly, we learn a lot from contrast. As view contrasting situations comparing one to another we see underlying lessons in each situation. If we can step into the witness state during the moments of polarity we can learn how to change. The brain registers the contrast that assists you in processing in new ways. From what seems to be tiny modifications that lead to huge changes in your life, these methods will get you there and assist you in manifesting in new ways. Now, it is up to you to get the ball rolling. Eventually, if you don't start making uplifting changes in your life, the whispers may turn into screams and a stronger experience may come your way.

Eleven Tips for Manifestation Results

1. **Write it!**
   - Write out your goals, your manifesting list.
   - Write a friend a future letter from you one year in advance. Write it as if you already have accomplished all of the things you want to accomplish now.
   - If you are in a group setting, then sit in the circle with the other members, who have done the prior two steps, and talk to them as if you are meeting again one year later from this day and tell them all that you have accomplished. This sets it in voice and mind as well as acting *as if*! You also have all of these friends in the circle being in what Denise Linn calls "Celebrate the Success of

Others". In being grateful for their success you are bringing it to you even faster as well. You bring your energy into an appreciation and gratifying vibration that raises you up and aligns you with the same and even better flow to you!

• Write a goal down that you desire on a piece of paper 15 times. Write out clearly what you desire and then write it again and again 15 times. This has been proven by millionaires. Put your emotions, feelings and ALL your senses into it. The more of your senses you can put into it the more powerful and speed with which it will manifest. You are putting your energy into it as you write it over and over again. Then release it!

2. Identify the Feeling

FEEL what you want to manifest. This in combination with using your body consistently every day it becomes a habit. So if you are passionate about becoming abundant, don't think about the how's. Don't think about how you will get there. Only think about how it will feel when you *are* there because as you feel it in the NOW (and because you can only create from the present moment) then you create the beam of magnetism to bring it to you. Feel it as if it already is and do it consistently! Consistency creates an expectancy in the brain and body which expands out to your entire being and continues to create from even a subconscious level. So create *good* habits. Ignite the feeling and create miracles in your life.

3. Build Your Energy

Whether you have received attunements to healing modalities or not, you can build your energy. We are all connected and One with Source. You only need to spend mere moments a day building your energy toward a miracle. Anything you choose will occur as you practice building your energy. Take a few deep breaths. Be with your breathing as it calms to a mere whisper. Close your eyes, be with yourself. State a prayer of connection and unity with your higher powers, as well as with your soul within. Call in the Angels for assistance.

Know that if you can imagine it, it will happen and even better than you can imagine. Start by visualizing the desired result. Start by being with the positive outcome. See beautiful lights of all colors surround you and your vision. You can first see pink unconditional love emanate throughout your entire being. Basking in a feeling of ever expanding love. Be within this energy and let it build. Bask in it. Warm delicious feelings surround you. Ever building. Then be with the brightest most assuredly divine white light that bursts into your vision and your entire being. Your soul cries with its beauty and power. Then you are in the place of knowing that you are deserving of all you desire. That the Universe is ALWAYS providing to you as that is exactly the purpose of creation. Build your energy every day towards clearing your energies, then being with your desires and put it to the Universe to assist you in your vibrational alignment. And so it is.

Meditate being centered and focused in just building energy. Visualizing an energy around you (your aura) and feeling it sparkling clean and clear and starting to build within you. You can focus on imagining feeling it until you really do. Your body may get warmer or feel chills. Your hands may get warmest of all depending on your own energy body. Practicing as often as possible will get your energy very high. Make it a regular routine. Sending, feeling and being Love to yourself and the world is the best way to manifest. Love energy is most powerful.

Basically, it's all about intention. Where your intention flows energy goes. So if you're asking to build your energy, you will. Also, in building your energy what assists that is keeping your chakras and aura clean, cleansed and cleared. There are many chakra balancing and energy clearing guided meditations out there or you can just do the meditation/visualization on your own as you flow into building energy. Another practice that is awesome for building energy is Qi Gong. They have wonderful exercises that work with your energy and the Universe's to help build. I felt it immediately even the first time I practiced. So much fun!

4. Awareness of Beliefs—Bee's Will

Did you know . . . Bee's can fly? But what Bee's don't know is . . . they can't fly. Or can they? According to scientific research (you may have heard) that, factually, Bee's should NOT be able to fly. Apparently, their wings are too small for their bodies and make it "impossible" for them to fly. However, since they do NOT "know" they "can't" fly, they DO. They fly because they have NO limits. There are no limiting beliefs.

And here is a fact that may or may not bear anything on what I've just said but I thought it was interesting. They've just discovered that bees have the same exact body structure as human but without the skeleton. Mmmm . . . .

Ever been told you can't do something and try as you might, you realize you can't. A determined person might prove that person wrong and DO IT. But then you see another person doing the same thing because they were never told they couldn't do it.

All our lives we are told we can't do it. But we CAN! Psychics are not unrealistic! What we expand our awareness on is an extra sense, the Sixth Sense (or ESP or psychic abilities) that scientists are only now expanding research on. Apparently, Mediumship abilities come from a certain part of the brain and other abilities another part of the brain and on and on. It seems that for every sense we have we expand that sense even broader and more open to the higher senses that were once "blocked" from us. I do not know the exact science of the matter, I just KNOW and Believe it exists and it works. It IS real and we CAN do it.

Do NOT Limit yourself. Do NOT NOT NOT listen to others who tell you it's impossible or who try to limit you even if they don't know it. It IS possible and you CAN do it. Time, practice and patience are a must. But remember to EXPECT it to happen, because it WILL. Sooner than you think!

One last reminder: Thought truly IS thing. If you think it, it will happen. So also, what you fear you will draw near. Do

NOT fear. Do NOT limit yourself, because it's only you that is stopping yourself from great things in your life. Just think positive, see the happy ending and it WILL happen. You can fly.

5. Always Be Grateful

Although I talk about gratitude at length in part two of this book, it is an essential part of manifesting so I will briefly lay this concept out here. We me be in a grateful state of mind now. Be grateful for what you have now. Be grateful for what you will have, as if it's already here. Expect it and then release it. Remember, if you are not feeling grateful you might be feeling resistance. And as they say, what we resist persists or what you fear you draw near. So do not focus on the negative things in your life, only the positive things. As you are in the positive state of mind you continue to bring positive experiences into your life. Whatever we resonate at is exactly what we receive. So raise your vibrations naturally and easily just by feeling grateful. Feel grateful for yourself, for your family, home, for your neighbors and co-workers and *their* good fortune too. As we are grateful to another's good fortune we assist in their continuing their good fortune. This is giving without expecting anything in return. And as we do that, we automatically are in a new vibration that feeds the positive energy and we receive that much faster and easier. So energize yourself and find those truly wonderful things to feel grateful for. As you do, you move to that place and transform. And you can manifest the life of your dreams.

It does take dedication, a positive outlook, forgiveness of self and others, and one thing that helped me (and I strongly suggest you do) is keep a Gratitude Journal. Write down ALL the good in your life. And I mean ALL the good. If you need to first get out all the bad, write it down, and then BURN that journal/paper. (This is very good for releasing all the bad once and for all. You're telling God you're not going to accept that ickiness in your life anymore.) Then EVERY DAY write down at least three things you are grateful for. (At least!) I know when I got started, I couldn't stop at 3. Do this for 21 days or more! After the 21 days, if you ever get in a funk do this exercise again. It works to adjust your brain waves to expecting more positive experiences to be grateful for and as you expect it, you align with that frequency and receive those positive experiences. Gratitude is one of the highest vibrations. Gratitude brings peace.

6. Clutter Clearing

This is like modern day alchemy. This has become very prominent in my life. I see it in my life and others' lives strongly. I know that as my environment changes, it emulates in my being. And so too when I change this emulates out into my environment. These seem to work together. Our personal environments are an expression of ourselves and what is inside of us. If you have a cluttered home or office, then there are things you need to clean up and clear within yourself. As you clean and clutter clear these areas the stagnant unmoving energy within you will also move. As I have cleansed myself and grown, my space has grown with me. And as you change your space you can see profound shifts within yourself. Make a conscious effort to make it happen now. Get rid of all things you don't need anymore!! If you don't use it or love it, get rid of it. It is clogging your energy. This lowers your vibration. You may have excuses like "maybe in the future" you will need it. By thinking this way and taking the action of saving these items you are affirming lack in your life and in your future. Get rid of it. The twist is that if you still subconsciously believe this may be needed and you get rid of it, the very next day you suddenly need that item. Know that you created that event. So know this ahead of time and you will cancel it out.

If you know it's a financial issue in question, go to the financial area in Feng Shui and clean the clutter there. If it's Relationship, go there and clean out clutter, etc. (A diagram of the Bagua is shown here. Use a ruler and divide your home into 9 even sections, as if looking at it from above. The front door is the front of the Bagua where Knowledge, Career and Helpful People sections are located.) If there are nurturing issues you can go to your kitchen and clean up in there. This is the nurturing room of the house. Our subconscious likes ritual and ceremonies. So go around the room either in body or mind and ask each item if it supports your energy or depletes you. If the energy feels good, keep it. If it feels low, then give it away or trash it. You may notice colors or lights or a memory attached to the item. If they give good feelings then keep it. If not, it's time to get rid of those items.

(Note for Hoarders: Hoarders have a different brain configuration. It's a biochemical challenge. Most hoarders do not know they have this. They can work with professionals to help them release this issue and can also get the help of their friends to rid them of clutter.)

7. Timing is Everything. So Allow!

This step is crucial to any manifesting results. Let the Universe work in its own way. Trust, faith, allow. LET IT GO! It will happen in its own time. We don't know the whole story. The universe has many intricacies to life. And remember, sometimes it's a good thing when some of our wishes and prayers are not granted. Sometimes, had we received our wish, our lives would not have taken a better course of action! So always be grateful and allow for divine timing and especially Divine surprises. Surrender everything to any particular outcome as your last step in manifesting. If you can't remain loose about the outcome and surrender to the end result then you are holding on to it too strongly. It will either not come at all or you will manifest it by way of control, but it will not be what it is meant to as the Divine wishes. You will be shown something you truly did not possibly need or veer off the tracks a bit. When you realize this you can get back on track. It's okay. We all do it sometimes. So allow for the magic and mystery of the Universe to unfold naturally. Hold out with optimism but remain loose and surrender.

8. Giving Uplifts You

Giving is a great way to manifest. If you truly give of your heart without expecting anything in return the feeling is unimaginable. Amazing. Giving without letting others know you were the one who did it is a higher feeling! This truly raises your vibrations. This deeply impacts your happiness and brings good to your life. So give giving a shot!

9. Vision (Seed) Board

These truly work miracles. Put everything on these beautiful creations that are all you. Be sure to include something that is YOU on the board so that the manifestations come to you. It can be a picture of you or a symbol that you feel represents you.

- Write out things you desire first.
- Get rubber cement, magazines (i.e. Oprah's O, etc.), Photos, Scissors
- Get very clear about what you want and why. What are the results you would like? Write on the back of collage what your intention is: "My intent is . . ." or "My desire . . ." and so on.

41

- Go for the feeling of what you want! Then get the images to match.
- Move them around till it feels right and glue
- Frame it
- Photograph it and reduce in size to keep it with you
- Place it where you will see it and your subconscious mind will get to reprogramming!
- You can also do this all in Microsoft PowerPoint or Adobe Photoshop if you're more into doing things online.

10. Manifest through FUN

Take the work out of it and only use the fun, positive, uplifting energy within you. I love to work with the faeries because they bring such lively fun energy to the table! When I work with them I know and realize all over again that I am one with them as they are one with me. We are all connected. I can imagine such fun with those little mini angels! They can fly about and get into such tiny places and do so many daring, lively and laugh out loud things that you can't help but smile when calling on them! I ask them to take their little wings and magic wands to fly about creating the miracles I request. Because I gain such upliftment from their energy and my own imagination working with them the miracles surface that much quicker, that much lighter, and that much more joyously! The Universe loves to work with positive uplifting vibrations. As you act from a fun place of being your frequency changes and raises to your more natural state of being. As you add more FUN to the picture of whatever it is you are manifesting, there is no work, only fun and the result comes quicker. Whenever you think there is work involved you won't do it or you might not stick with it for long. But life is worth living! Life is meant to be lived and loved and be filled with laughter and happiness! Do whatever it takes to make it fun and happy! That is where your truest passion exists and has the highest potential for success!

11. Take ACTION

You can't manifest by sitting and visualizing and being in the positive energies alone. We are here for a reason. We are here to listen to the Divine and express by way of our bliss. We must listen to our intuition after we put a request out there to the Universe and take those actions steps necessary. Although a lot of things will come to you just by way of your intention alone there will still be certain action steps for most things. These things will require your active energy to follow through and take action. Simply listen to the whispers and follow your heart.

Chapter 5

Signs, Signs, Everywhere There Are Signs

S igns, Serendipities, Synchronicities, "coincidences" are all
names for messages and guidance from a higher source and
from within. There truly are no coincidences. That word implies
that an experience is random and has no meaning. When truly
all experiences happen for a reason and all experiences have
meaning. It just depends on how awake and aware you are to
noticing them. Not to mention the paradox that you can assign
a meaning to anything or nothing at all. It is up to you if you
find meaning in something. It is up to your consciousness and
your level in vibration if something is random, happen-stance,
or something more for your life, or simply IS. Sometimes there
is further meaning as a guidance system from beyond that you
can listen to and take action from. Sometimes there is no action
to be taken. And sometimes the lesson truly is to simply let it
be and your action is actually *no action* or stillness. Sometimes
you simply are meant to be in a certain space to hold the space

as a silent observer, simply witnessing and not attaching any meaning to anything, anywhere and simply BE. Be in bliss and joy. This is something you can do in any situation whether there is divine action to be taken or not.

Dr. Carl Jung deserves most of the credit for developing the concept of synchronicities. Signs are one of my favorite awakening symptoms of them all! (More on awakening symptoms in Book Two, *Divine Embrace*.) This is one of the first symptoms that people become aware of upon waking up; from the unconscious life to conscious living. Your awakening starts with many synchronistic events; events that are patterns of a small or large scale. As you become more aware you realize you are guided. You have always been guided and always will be. Some common signs are seeing animals or numbers. There are symbolic meanings to the guidance animals and numbers bring. Look them up as they show up in your life to find what resonates with you.

Many will see patterns of numbers in a row or many times a day. The most common is seeing the numbers 11:11 on your clock or wherever you are. This is a way of triggering something within your system that allows you to question your surroundings and wake up. 11:11 is also the gateway number that tells you that you are opening up. A good sign. I often see 777 or 444. I hear that 444 is the Angel number and 777 is the Angels laughing with happiness at where you are at or what you've just done. There are many books out there you can read to help you with number synchronicities. Such as Doreen Virtue's *Angel Numbers 101*. Many books and websites will have varying messages for number sequences and they may be completely different messages. So something you'll notice is that whatever book, website or information you run into about the number sequences you look up are the messages you needed to hear on that day. Whatever you feel the number means truly is what it means and what you are meant to follow for that moment. For me, I don't always know the number sequence meaning and I'm not always drawn to look them up. My first trigger is that I have noticed this synchronicity and the Universe is speaking to me, letting me know it's alive and guiding me. If I am ever drawn to look up the meaning, then I am meant to know a little more and whatever I find that is what I am meant to know for that day.

When animals come into your life they bring with them a message for you. It may be in the way you have met them or something more deeply that you can ponder by looking up their meaning in books such as my favorite *Animal Speak* by Ted Andrews. They may be your totem animal, an animal that is your spiritual guide for a short time or for life. If you are willing to listen and hear their message they can guide you in your life. I like to get things in threes, so if an animal is coming to you three times or more definitely sit up and take notice. Find out what they have to say for you. You can take a soul journey within during meditation and talk with your animal messenger. You can meet them in a sacred place and find out what messages they have to share with you. You may be surprised at our link with animals.

It's quite common during a spiritual awakening, especially a Kundalini awakening to see snakes everywhere you go. The serpent represents our spinal column or Sushumna channel in Kundalini, our divine life force energy. I usually come across garden snakes or references and pictures of them in books and online. This, for me, is a continued confirmation that I am on the right Kundalini pathway for me and waking up through Kundalini Shakti.

Why just today I went for a walk on the trails near my work. It's nice and private and I'm usually the only one walking them when I go. (I usually avoid the lunch rush and go before or after. Today it was after.) A deer ran out onto my path RIGHT in front of me! So close and still so quiet and graceful. Then I rounded the corner it ran off to and it was still there. She had stopped and turned her head to look at me. I kept walking towards her and said, "Hi" with a smile. Not sure why but wanted to and she still stayed there looking at me as I walked closer and closer. When I was maybe 5-7 feet away she took off again while still looking at me like she wanted to say something or do something. Then she went off in the woods. I walked into the woods as well (on the path though) and then turned around where I usually do about 30 feet up and walked back where I came from. And then I saw her again out in the open on a grassy path, off the path I was on and she seemed to be perusing for food or just walking. She didn't seem to notice me this time but I don't think my presence scared her. That was cool. Three Deer sightings in five minutes time.9 (I know same deer but it came in three's. And I'm big on three's.)

So I perused online for a symbolic meaning, of which, I found a beautiful meaning of abundance, gentle grace, compassion and love. Sometimes when you read the meaning of animals you will be bombarded with information. Take whatever stands out the most. But don't ignore the uncomfortable. Sometimes that's exactly what you need to read and understand. So simply notice as the neutral witness what stands out as a message for you. Overall, animals always remind me of the magic in our natural world. They always give me a message of coming back to presence, simplicity, bliss and grace.

There are events that are synchronistic as well that you will notice. Bumping into people that you were just thinking about. Having something easily handed to you just when you needed it most. A sequence of events that leads to something truly profound and amazing. This is sometimes attached to a déjà vu feeling. The list can go on forever. These serendipitous events are your sign that you are waking up and that your life is guided. That more you sit back and become aware of your surroundings the more you will notice this guidance. As you listen you will receive even more guidance during your life. Always assisting you to get back to the divine being you always were and already are. :)

The more you start to work with the Law of attraction, the more you will start to notice the signs all around you. And the more signs that will come to you due to this new awareness.

Now test the Universe! You can test it and it will answer! Send a request to receive a sign back from the Universe at least three times. Try it with a Flower. I chose a purple flower because I love the color purple. I asked the Universe to bring me a Purple Flower (with my mind, but feel free to do it out loud if that helps you, it also adds to the energy). Now this could show up in MANY forms. Not just an actual flower, but maybe you see a picture of one, or maybe you hear a reference to it in a story, as was the case with me.

I asked and then a few days later I came back into work, checked my hotmail account. I'm on a psychic/paranormal e-group and a member posted that she just recently added a story to her ghost story page on her website, she told us all to check it out and that it had to do with a flower. So of course I had to go look and see if it was my purple flower. As I read the story it did in fact mention a purple flower, purple being the favorite color of the person who sent the flowers to the narrator of the story. So there was my request from the Universe, my purple flower. Of course I wasn't happy with only a REFERENCE to a purple flower. So I put that thought out there again (this time with more detail) and asked for a REAL Purple flower.

I must have put this thought out there too many times! I was upset over something a few days after this request and my sister came home with an arrangement of many different kinds of purple flowers for me! During this week, my niece also brought in hand-picked purple flowers.

Now it's your turn! See what turns up. If you put the energy out there for something and do not fear against the thought (thereby putting thought into it NOT happening), this *will* happen. You have to think it, and then KNOW it and it WILL happen. Again, it's always debatable if what happens from your thought is only happening because it was meant to happen. Although I do believe everything happens for a reason. It's possible that you were meant to find the Universe and know this knowledge of energy and thereby making things happen for you for the better. Try not to over-think it!

These signs ring our bells and assist us in tuning in! In seeing these signs and recognizing them for the magical qualities that they are, you also link yourself to the Divine. You feel a stronger connection to the Divine Source and that you are a special part of the All. And as you wake up to this divine connection you are unstoppable and all-powerful! You can remove dis-ease even before it starts, you can manifest divine experiences, you can feel happy more often, you can be more of the you that you truly are and always wanted to be but thought you couldn't do it or thought you weren't deserving or thought it was only for someone else to have or thought it was never possible. But wait, it truly is and it starts from waking up and see those synchronicities in your life.

Even after years of recognizing these signs and synchronicities it's easy to fall back into dull non-feeling mode and forget. So you need to get back on track and wake up, consciously choose to see those signs, see them occurring right now! Expect the magic that occurs in EVERY DAY. No matter if the sun is shining or not. No matter what experience is happening in your life right now. No matter the drama. No matter the outside happenings. The magic is there. It is not hidden from you. It is right out there in the open waiting for you to see it. Take notice! The more you recognize them, the more they show up. The more you recognize the power within you. You feel that divine connection that's always been there and was simply waiting for you to really SEE it.

As you start to see the world for the magical place that it is, you connect more completely to your divine higher self, your spark from within. And as you do this you raise your vibrations, align with your light body and move more fully into the light being you are. Enjoy the simplicity and magic that signs from the Divine bring you every day. The enchanting pull from serendipities allows you to flow with the musical ocean of life.

Chapter 6

Reality Shifts

Reality Shifting can be described in a few different ways depending on your perspective. I'm going to preface this and say I am not a scientist and have no drive to research science behind things. However, I do so appreciate those that take the time to do this, so that folks like me can benefit from their research! Let's first start by explaining that our soul's have a soul signature. This signature is a vibration that has a number, a color, a sound and more that make up our vibration or frequency. It's a vibration or frequency that we as energy beings always resonate at. This frequency changes throughout our lives as we grow and evolve through our experiences.

For me reality shifting is like manifesting. Since this reality is but an illusion we've created, reality shifts can occur by our very own wishes/vibration and that of group consciousness vibration and that of mass consciousness as vibration well. So the one has the power and the many have the power. It is within us all. It is like Neo in the Matrix. If you haven't watched it, he comes to a crossroads where he can take one of two pills. Which pill do you choose? The one that keeps you in the safe unconscious place you are still in? Or the one that wakes you up to true reality and truly living. I've chosen the latter. If you're reading this, chances are you have too. It may take time. But simply by being open and asking the 'What if it was true?' question you are allowing the truth to blossom within you.

Have you ever noticed when an object has been moved or disappeared? Only to reappear again in a new spot or even the same spot you already checked! Have you ever been able to get a parking spot in the same exact spot you "requested" time and again? This is a talent for manifesting. Have you felt time speed up or slow down? Shifting reality happens whether we're paying attention to it or not. Though it seems when we pay attention to it, it happens more often (or maybe it's just our awareness expanding).

We are all energy beings. What we feel we put out to the Universe and thus the request is made and it comes back to us. What we are feeling now is putting energy into our future (and if you can wrap your mind around this: even into our past and present). There seems to be parallel Universes to this one where there are a variety of paths we can choose. If we are presented with a situation, we will then create a variety of different responses to that situation (many paths to choose). If we choose one way, we are creating, following and choosing that Universe. Our other choices will fall into the other parallel Universes playing themselves out in those separate realities. Like many forks in the road, we choose one path for one choice and that takes us in one direction. The other paths are still playing out their "movies" in a parallel Universe (another "You"). A great movie that gives you the best visual for this is "Next" with Nicolas Cage. The goal here is to truly feel positive, peaceful, loving and happy in order to put *that* request out to the Universe to receive positive, peaceful, loving and happy experiences/reality shifts/manifestations. At least I assume the majority would like to feel peaceful, positive and happy. It's always your choice! Free will!

Johnny from "The Dead Zone" (if you believe this fictional television show as real in this example) causes Reality Shifts every episode after he receives his visions. In one episode Johnny received a vision of a possible outcome where a train station blows up in the very near future. After receiving the lifelike vision Johnny then prevents the explosion at the train station. We then see how he changes the outcome to something more positive. If this were real, you can come to a conclusion that the power of Johnny's and his partner's convictions caused a change in the energy—a shift. You can also assume the possibility that all of the people at the train station even subconsciously (or their soul's) decided on having a better outcome. Coming out of the victim mode, no longer needing to feel a bad experience therefore changed their energy to feeling an experience of a higher vibration, the happier more positive outcome. Where all those go home with the ones they love, others make new relationships with ones they just met and so on. The other not-so-great reality may live out in another parallel universe. We make choices every day to which reality we will choose to live out—minute by minute, second by second. My goal is to keep my vibration as high as possible and in line with the highest possible positive reality I can achieve.

Raising your vibration is prudent in receiving higher more positive results. Whatever you receive to you is an EXACT match to what you put out to the Universe in vibration. It's a mirror of what you currently are vibrating at. Just like Abraham-Hicks states, "You are always living a reflection of whatever you are outputting. And so, if you get into a little pocket where a lot of people are being rude, it's probably because you are being rude—or because you have been aware of people being rude. Nothing ever happens to you that is not part of your vibration!"

Remember to, cleanse and clear your energies (chakras and aura) daily. Even by simply reminding yourself that you are 100% perfect whole and complete snaps you back into a whole and complete higher vibrational state. And in a pinch white light is fast and easy to visualize filling you up and clearing you out. It is God energy and that is what you are made of.

Pay attention to what experiences, people and feelings you are feeling at this VERY MOMENT, because that is what you are vibrating at. If you don't like what you are seeing, CHANGE IT. FEEL GOOD! Receive positive results. I've discussed more powerful guidelines in raising your vibration previously in this chapter.

Over time, you may notice when you are raising your vibration higher and higher that eventually it's easy to just flow with the waves of life. That you will actually just smoothly flow through life just like waves from the ocean. There is no effort required, just being. Taking what comes happily and seeing things come more easily to you. Truly feeling free. As is explained in the way of the Tao and most recently superbly interpreted by Wayne Dyer in his latest book called *Changes your thoughts, Change your life: Living the Wisdom of the Tao*.

There is a superb website that explains in wonderful detail Reality Shifting and many other attributes. Cynthia Sue Larson is the owner of Reality Shifters and explains this phenomenon in easy to comprehend terms here: www.RealityShifters.com. Check it out!

The Guitar Pick

I would like to give a few examples of Reality Shifting (or manifesting). The first is from beyond the grave. This happened to me and is my very own validation into reality shifting, manifesting, energy and living on the Other Side, and the Universe as a whole:

Michael died on November 13th 1990. I was devastated. He was that unique person at school that everyone loved. He made the room smile just with his presence. Michael died just 8 days after his 16th birthday. In the year 2000 I started to finally recognize signs from Michael combined with signs for 13's and didn't know what the connection was!? I was perplexed except for his Date of Death being on the 13th. Thanksgiving in 2002, a friend gave me a reading (she is very good in her mediumship). She really felt that Michael wanted me to visit his grave when I went to visit my parents in upstate New York on Thanksgiving. I definitely planned on visiting his grave anyway, but for some reason didn't get to do it. No time. But I visited again two months later in January 2003. I went to Michael's gravesite at that time. I wanted to buy Michael a mini-guitar to put by his grave, but couldn't find any small enough, so I ended up buying him a purple guitar pick; one for him and an identical one for me. I pulled up to the front of the cemetery, and as you must know it snows often in upstate New York during the winter. Well, Michael's area in the cemetery was sectioned off and NOT PLOWED! But I was determined, as I missed visiting him in November (when it hadn't snowed as much yet, another reason for the hint from Michael to go two months prior rather than in January). So I climbed over the barrier and trenched through the three feet of snow to his grave. Then came the REAL challenge.

Michael has a flat grave on the ground!? I knew his stone was between two little trees. There were THREE MORE like that around his grave. So I did what ANY SANE person would do in this situation! I started kicking and digging snow out of the way. I finally got to the THIRD one and there he was. I dug two areas before I found his. It was important to me to see his grave with his name and the etched in guitar on his stone. Also because I had brought him a purple guitar pick to put by his grave (he loved his guitar). I dug a little in the frozen ground, placing the guitar pick in as much as I could. Knowing it would eventually be gone, but I kind of felt like I knew he'd grab it for himself. I had a vision while I was there kneeling, almost sitting in the pile of snow behind me, of Michael coming and giving me flowers. ME! And I'm the one visiting HIS grave. :) So then I trudged through the snow back to my car.

Almost three years after I left that guitar pick in the frozen ground for Michael, I decided to visit my parents in upstate NY again and brought my son with me. This time it was spring-time. As a part of my visit I took both my son and I to visit Michael's grave. It was nice to visit his grave without trudging through the snow this time. I pulled my car right up next to where his grave is. As my son was preparing to get out I was already walking to his grave and looking down to see his name and date of death. To my complete shock, I not only saw the familiar head stone but also the purple guitar pick I left him almost three years prior!! I must add here that I did visit his grave after that initial trip and before this one. Nothing was there at those times!! The guitar pick was resting right on the head stone, as if waiting for me. It's like he held on to it for a while and then gave it to me at a time he felt I needed extra faith. I took the guitar pick with me to prove to others that I now had two, instead of one, guitar pick. However, I realized I didn't need to prove anything to anyone. I experienced this myself and I believe. I brought the guitar pick back to Michael's grave and said thank you!

I still have my guitar pick and carry that pick around in my purse! Amazing! Spirit can manifest material possessions as well as signs for us. Michael did just that for me! To this day I still see signs from Michael letting me know he is still around and always there for me.

We Would Have Never Met

The next reality shift is how my Husband shifted his consciousness one day and on that very same day set up the fated day for us to meet. So we probably would not have met if he didn't shift his consciousness and say "enough" of this lower vibrational way of being. The story has him working at a restaurant where he worked for eleven years. He had the opportunity to start a web design busy where he would set up clients with websites. He was sitting on this opportunity for a bit. But one day, he finally got sick of where he was and what he was doing with his life. He said, "Enough!" He realized he can have so much more. He gave his two weeks notice to the restaurant where he worked and went on foot to find clients. It was a few stops later where he walked into the metaphysical shop I worked out of. I wasn't there at the time. The owner let him know that she already had a web design (who was me at the time) and that I did require some assistance and would love to barter a healing session with him (his first) in trade for his assistance on the website. He agreed and our first meeting was his first healing session on the very day of the Summer Solstice and full moon combined. When I met him I knew he would be my Husband. Is it a coincidence that mine and Don's "song" just came on as I write this? I say no way. In case you were wondering, our song is *You and Me* by Lifehouse. ☺

Determination

This reality shift reminds me of my last example. The story is from a couple I met at my Soul Coaching retreat with Denise Linn. This couple is my inspiration! The man, a very kind Polish man with a thick accent. The woman, a spunky, loving American interior designer. You would never have put the two together if you met them separately. But together they are a power couple in energy and love. So the story is that he met with a psychic one day where she told him he would meet the "one" but not for eight years. He was very disappointed at hearing this. At the end of the reading she said, "There is always free will." This stuck with him. That evening he said, "No way!" (shift in consciousness you think!?) and right then and there told his angels he is ready now and intends to be with his "one" now. The very next day he went to a workshop and sat right next to this woman!!! They really evolved into the beautiful couple they are and even got married a few months after the Soul Coaching retreat I met them at.

*   *   *

The reason I bring these last two reality shifting stories up is because both times each person said, "No way! Enough!" and a shift occurred in their consciousness to something better, a new reality . . . . maybe. A higher vibrational merge into an evolved way of being . . . maybe.

Make the Shift

So now, it's your turn if you so choose. So if there is any leeway it seems that it is up to us to make that shift. Mind you, sometimes it's not going to require nor will it be necessary for a huge shift within yourself to occur consciously for a shift to actually happen. Sometimes all that is required of you is to remember to remain in your peace and bliss within. As long as you have that then each challenge that comes will flow and move through you. And sometimes rather than sitting with a challenge something inside of you may surge and an inner divine guidance system will tell you that it's time for you to make a conscious shift and say "no more" to something and raise your vibrations. Once you wake up to an imbalance or challenge you are aware of its existence and have the power to change it. We see it and now we can change it.

Shift your conscious through consistency, an open heart, and positive thinking throughout the day! Even when you don't want to or ESPECIALLY when you don't want to, **CHANGE your thought.** Throughout the day just periodically check-in with your thoughts. What are you thinking RIGHT NOW? Do you want this thought to create your future? What we are doing in this very moment is creating our future.

We all need those reminders. Making a **conscious decision** to read or hear something spiritual or uplifting on a daily basis is crucial to staying in the upward spiral of positive energy flow. Read for a few minutes an uplifting spiritual book or listen to a positive CD, etc. The more you remind yourself when you are in those lower moments to think positive, be positive, feel positive, do something positive in order to get yourself out of that lower vibrational moment, the less those lower vibrational moments will show up. You will condition your subconscious into a new way of being. Absolutely Divine!

In order to get down deep into our subconscious mind we must remember our every day thoughts and beliefs bury into our subconscious. So even if we start to think positive and act as if we are happy, we will need to get down deep for it to take a permanent hold in our daily lives through the subconscious mind. Listening to positive meditations that have positive subliminal messages is a great method to shift your subconscious. Hypnosis and daily affirmations are other time proven methods. These methods will assist you in manifesting more positive results from your desires as well as naturally attract to you more uplifting experiences.

You need to MOVE. Move your body. When you feel that low vibration or negative feelings, GET UP and MOVE! Walk away IMMEDIATELY or you will get into a downward spiral. Get **outside** for even just a few minutes. **BREATHE** and relax into just BEING. I'd say consciously doing this every hour on the hour is prudent for all of us. If getting up, at first, is not possible, stop what you are doing and just BREATHE. Breathe deeply, close your eyes and see the SUN on your face. Imagine the warmth and good feelings. FEEL GOOD NOW. It can happen as quickly as that if you allow it. Enjoy this new way of being in every moment. Be in the NOW **RIGHT NOW**.

Trust and Faith are key factors. We must also let go of situations that seem out of our control. If there is something that is happening and you do not like it, try your best not to think negatively about it. Let out your feelings then immediately CHANGE it. Immediately take your POWER back from the situation and visualize positive outcomes. FEEL that outcome as better and the way YOU want it and it WILL be. You create ALL experiences that come to you. We are NO LONGER victims of our circumstances. We NEVER were. We've always created what has happened to us in our lives. NOW we can consciously create better higher vibrational positive outcomes! It's OUR choice now. What do you choose?

Then have **FAITH** that all will work out as it should. Know that you are always taken care of by the Universe. Know that your request has been heard, don't worry or think on the "How's", just focus on the end result and FEEL GOOD NOW! When you take that weight off your shoulders and let God do the walking, you can rest, relax and be in the moment and feel good. It is time for us to be in the energy of RECEIVING (the energy of the Feminine). The masculine has been more pronounced throughout the years and now we are receiving more support from the Feminine, the act of just being and receiving support allow the Universe to bring it to you more easily. Just sit back and let it come. Trust and be in the flow. Feel open and good now and it comes to you more easily.

And sometimes we must evaluate what we are doing. If we are banging our heads against the wall and still doing the same things over and over again, we must face facts, take our ego-voice out of the equation and realize that there is something we are still doing that we should not be doing, or something that we are missing that we need to start doing.

Meditating is strongly recommended to listen to your TRUE voice and not that of the ego. We all have a hard time deciphering what is our ego and what is our true inner voice/our soul. Your ego will be pushy, negative and demanding. Your true inner soul's voice will just feel right, be a gentle guiding voice and always consistent with its message. It is patient and will keep sending you gentle nudges along the way till you listen. We have FREE WILL so it is up to us to listen to our ego's or our inner soul's voice.

Don't get me wrong, the ego serves a lovely purpose in protecting us and helping us to wake up to something we are not seeing. By sending us lower vibrational feelings of guilt, hate, jealousy and fear, your ego may protect you from delving deeper into a situation. However, over the many years our ego has taken over. It doesn't want to be easily squashed. We can thank the ego when those feelings arise and release it. Peel that layer of the onion away (or as the donkey in the movie "Shrek" prefers to say, peel the layers of chocolate cake away). As you peel away those layers your inner voice becomes stronger. We've all experienced our inner voice and when we are listening our lives unfold before us in such positive and magical ways, as if all on its own. It's much easier and our lives have balance.

The Law of Attraction and the Law of Allowing are key factors to receive magical reality shifts in your life! Reality shifting happens in many forms. It's a magical way of living life if you allow. Just ask the Universe to give you more experiences and the Universe will provide. It is Universal Law.

Chapter 7

Law of Giving—Pay It Forward

We now come to the Universal Law of Giving. This is also what we've already briefly mentioned as one essential key to manifesting. Give and you shall receive. This is meaning of the **Law of Giving**. When you start to consciously manifest, know that **you receive that which you give, multiplied.** Watch what happens when you give something away. Selflessly give anything away without the expectation of anything in return. You will see it come back to you multiplied. For example, you decide to give away $40 to someone in need. You think nothing of it, but only to service a fellow human being. That week or even on the same day the circle happens and you've received something of worth or actual cash that is $120 or even more. It is always the same or more than what you gave out.

Also, it does depend on if you are counteracting any negative poverty thinking with positive thoughts and feelings. If you are thinking you are poverty stricken, you may cancel out the Law of Giving. You will still receive multiples of what you gave out. So it is beneficial to stop giving out the frequency vibration of poverty or lacking in any way. Wash away those thoughts and allow the natural way of giving and receiving to occur in your life.

Exercise is the best analogy for this law. When you first start exercising it might seem cumbersome. Over time you feel more energized. You will notice even on the same day that after you've exercised you actually have *more* energy not less. When exercising you are first putting forth more of your energy in order to produce even more energy. So first you give energy and then you get more! This is law. Our bodies work this way and so too does the world outside of ourselves.

Giving and living in service is natural and organic. It is the way of the ancients. This way of living is what's missing from our connection. Now giving with the selfish notion of receiving something in return is not going to get you results. You must simply want to give to feel the art of giving kindly to another. It might start out as a feeling of being forced from within. However, once you start it seems to really feel good and better than had you been the one receiving. You notice happy faces from those you service. You see the positive results and are genuinely happy to service them for *their* good will and good fortune. It's a feeling from inside of you, your energy and vibration that tells you when you are in alignment with selfless giving. This vibration attracts more good to you. Suddenly you are caught up in a powerful blissful state of giving. As you are there you effortless receive all that you could ever want or need from the Divine. It is law.

Now don't go putting yourself into the poor house because you want to give to the many in need! You might have a big heart and really want to share with everyone. However, you don't want to put yourself in the poor house by not giving wisely. You might end up putting yourself into a position where you can't give anymore if you go overboard. Not to mention you will eventually grow tired and resent the charities and needy people for taking all your time and effort away. Mostly you will be hard on yourself for having done too much for too many for too long. In regards to money, take a percentage (say 10%) of your salary that you can designate to give to another. In regards to time, give only a balanced amount of your time that still allows you to have proper rest, proper fun time, proper family time, and so on. Everything in moderation. Even when giving. If we all gave of ourselves in moderate balanced proportions this world would be in such a higher more beautiful state of being right now! So bring balance to your life while seeing where you can lend a helping hand.

Have you ever watched the movie *Pay It Forward*? The movie is amazing; the concept Divine. In *Pay It Forward* the star, 7th grade boy, Trevor (played by Haley Joel Osment) receives an extra credit assignment to change the world. Taking this assignment seriously Trevor devises a beautiful plan he calls "Pay It Forward". The idea is that it starts with one person and spans out. One person will give selflessly one good deed to three people. The only thing asked in return is that those three people also do one good deed to three more people. This giving isn't always something that is comfortable for the giver but it is a selfless act. The Universe seems to divinely place into each participants laps people in need of what they can selflessly give. As you can see, if all participants actively partake in this game the giving is insurmountable!

Think about it. If we all did that life on Earth might shift a little more, be a little more peaceful, feel more in balanced. Well, until we all get there, we can at least strive for this in our own lives and allow it to spread naturally. And it will. Like wild fire.

You must do your best to live in the higher vibrations and raise your frequency. By living an honest life filled with integrity and meaning. Following your bliss as well. And doing what works best for your mind, body and soul. Listening to the inner messages of your soul to do what it is asking. Not putting lower vibrational substances in the body is helpful (at least not often). Not being around people that make you feel down and low in energy. Not hanging around places that make you feel down. Then taking it one step further and going after what feels good. Get outside often. Out in nature we are in our element and breathe in the natural prana life force energy. The sun gives this to us naturally. Move the body every day to work out the stagnancy. Eat what lifts your bodies energies. Our bodies are always speaking to us so listen up! :) *And if you want to take it one step further, do a good deed or two. This will boost your mood AND your immune system as well as the receivers! :)*

I challenge you to make a New Years resolution that gives every day 365 days a year. Each and every day see if there is something that you can give of yourself to another. Something to share or a light to shine upon another. Seek to either give:

- Words of Encouragement;
- Time; and/or
- Resources (Money, Clothing, a Service)

Fact: Giving an act of kindness, receiving an act of kindness or witnessing an act of kindness lifts your serotonin levels and boosts your immune system!!! That's HUGE. It's a win win on both sides. We are made from the Eyes of the Divine. ☺

Chapter 8

Law of Karma

The Law of Karma plays an integral and deeply embedded part in our lives. So what is karma to me and what have I felt from it to this point? The inner workings of Karma is something that is often debated. It seems to be one of those things that evolves in its true meaning as we ascend. Karma is the recording of service or action taken. And by action taken I am meaning that action taken out of desire. If there is action taken out of selfless service this is a divine higher way of taking action that is karma-less; pure; Divine. Karma is recorded for actions of love, caring, compassion, generosity, sincerity and kindness, as well as for killing, harming for advantages, taking more than is needed, acting on desires. Simply having desires creates karma. Or rather, it's having the attachments to those desires that create karma. You are in the realm of creating and therefore create karma and staying in the recycling of lives.

When you become pure of mind and desireless, then you are free of attachments and free of karma. Here you ascend.

When we act on desires we also attract its opposite. As said in the Bhagavad Gita: A Walkthrough for Westerners by Jack Hawley, the opposite of our desires is anger. With every action out of desire suffering ensues. Even simply eating for the pure pleasure of it is a desire that will bring suffering. A lesson I have and continue to learn. Having been 90 pounds overweight with an overeating issue, I can attest to this particular example. But when we come back to only eating what our body needs we are in balance with life.

You can take action and not create Karma. That action is the desireless selfless action. When there is nothing desired as a gain from an action, this is selfless service. Giving it all up to the Divine is vitally important. Simply acting with selfless service, always giving it up to the Divine wipes out karmic debt and allows you to stop the cycle of birth, death and rebirth. Knowing who you truly are is key here. Your true essence, the Divine, is not in the positive or negative of life. It is beyond all of that and it does not create life nor is affected by it. It simply is. It's the true essence that which you are and the goal of which you are to know. Our highest goal in life is to learn who we truly are, to move beyond attachments, desires, positive and negative experiences, and to simply know who we are from within and come back to that Source connection.

Samskara's are deeply stored imprints from actions and desires asleep in the unconscious. Once they are active, they produce the desires and result in actions creating more karma. So here you know the goal is to not accumulate more karma but to release those unconscious actions and desires before they become active and to stay in a neutral non-dual state of being. In a non-dual state of being you are in pure bliss and peace. You are in the in-between, the middle path, or void. Nothing that occurs is good or bad. It simply Is. You do not attach yourself to the experience or the outcome. You simply observe in your beautiful true state of being. You get out of attracting more karma to you while you complete the process of releasing the old karma already accumulated. Once it is integrated and transmuted a beautiful Oneness state of being is your result. Remember as you are in a higher, peaceful, uplifted state of being only higher, peaceful, uplifting experiences are naturally attracted to you anyway.

So an example of karma would be if you deliberately did something bad or negative to someone, like knowingly cutting someone off in traffic just to get ahead, you will in turn receive that same level of negative or malicious back to you and not necessarily from the same person or the same exact event. Likewise, if you did something positive for someone else, like helping someone carry their groceries into their house, you have created and will receive a like positive experience to that nature. Timing is not always immediate and it can take a while to receive things especially if you feel you are undeserving and thereby using the law of attraction to receive nothing positive your way. But it is law so when you move your being into a more positive state and know you are deserving the positive karma has room to express itself to you. However, remember that if you are doing these acts simply as a way to be self-serving and receive more good in your life then you are still caught in the cycle of Karma; birth, death and rebirth. However, if you doing these wonderful acts of assisting others without a desired outcome and giving it all up to the Divine, not attaching to the outcome, then you will stay in a state of your true connection to Source and out of the karmic cycle. Give it all up to the Divine and know your True self.

Another thought came to me when chatting about Karma with a guest our radio show (my Husband and I). I wondered of examples such as what if the person did something that inadvertently affected another but it was not their intent to do any harm. For example, if a person was driving the speed limit and another person behind them came out of know where in a rush and aimed their negative thoughts their way. Or if someone was the target of venom even though they never did anything to that other person. Such as if a boy broke up with a girl and the boy got a new girlfriend. The old girlfriend may aim venom towards the new girlfriend even though she had nothing to do with the break up. These examples seem to be the person who is aiming the venom creating new karma, negative karma, that will come back to bite them later and they will be the target of venom later on. And since things tend to come full circle, it's also possible these people that have obliviously become targets have in times past (even past or other lives) had started a karmic circle that was then coming back to bite *them* even if they didn't really do anything this time. It was what they did in times past that caused this to come back to them. You never can tell. Which is why it's so healthy to step back and remember: It's not good. It's not bad. It just is. Then take yourself out of further Karma cycles. By removing yourself from creating more Karma you end that cycle. When you stay free of creating positive or negative cycles of Karma you finish off whatever is left of what was created and live in more peace. This is said to also remove you from further being incarnated into future lives as well. We can't help what someone else is doing or feeling but we *can* help how we feel or react.

Karma cleansing is to clean the bad karma. There are some folks that can go to the Akashic record of the soul to transform the karma. A master, like Master Dr. Sha (quoted below), gives people the power to enlighten themselves; to help the souls. A Master can move away the suffering of the soul. To clear only the body is not enough. It is the body, mind **and** soul. Some Masters will use shaktipat, which is an energetic transmission performed by an enlightened master (this is like one powerful source of Divine energy charging another with a cleansing affect) and some will cut karma cords with visualizations and energy and many others will use a variety of other methods. A shaktipat assists in spiritual awakening. This is an infusion of energy from the spiritual master to the seeker. Shaktipat brings about the awakening of the seeker's own inherent spiritual power, called Kundalini.

Karma cleansing can happen through consciously working on your blockages and patterns and removing them from your life for a better way. Karma cleansing can occur via Shaktipat as well. Gurumayi Chidvilasananda of www.siddhayoga.org talks of this, "Shaktipat is described by the yogic texts as an initiation that activates an inner unfolding of awareness that leads to progressively higher states of consciousness. Over time, through grace and our efforts in spiritual practice, the sense of separation from divinity drops away. We come to recognize the presence of God in ourselves and in the world around us. We experience the world as a play of God's energy."

What we are doing here in this book is a way of starting the cleansing process or working through the process if you've already started. Depending on where you are in your evolvement will depend on what profound changes will occur within you.

Dr. Zhi Gang Sha of www.soulmastersmovie.com talks of his beliefs on the subject, "People talk about mind over matter, the power of the mind. But I think the power of the mind is not enough. The next step is soul over matter, the power of the soul. Everyone and everything has a soul. The soul can heal. Heart touch heart, soul touch soul."

Release. We seem to release in layers. And a little more gets shaved off the top. More blockages are removed. Something that comes up might come up again in a new way. You go deeper. It is simply allowing you to release slowly and at your pace so you have a balanced awakening. If you removed it all at once you might go crazy. Take time. It's a balanced progression to awaken. Even with awakening there must be moderation and balance. Heaven is always within you now. There's no where to go but here. So enjoy the ride as you get "there" or rather here.

Part II

Steps to True Inner Peace

Chapter 9

Steps to True Inner Peace
Introduction

"Without Inner Peace it is impossible to have World Peace."
~ Dalai Lama

True Inner Peace comes from within. Come to the core essence of your being. Reduce external and internal clutter of the mind. Learn how to connect, expand and awaken your inner spark. You can remain centered in your true self no matter what occurs around you. This quote says it best (author unknown), "Peace. It doesn't mean to be in a place where there is no noise, trouble or hard work. It means to be in the midst of those things and still be calm in your heart." As you connect to Source you come from a place of neutrality and peace. When you do this you raise the vibrations of your surroundings and the planet. Thus, a natural spiritual and Kundalini awakening occurs within you.

Along with utilizing all the Laws of the Universe that you read in part 1, this section focuses on elements and guidelines that assist you along your path to self-realization. These are things that have come naturally to me along my path. Each of these elements have truly assisted in a peaceful balanced awakening thus far for me. You can work with these guidelines as much as possible to transcend peacefully. Of course, remember take what you like and leave the rest!

Finding True Inner Peace is as simple as drawing out the clutter in our outer reality and the clutter we allow in our inner reality. Inner peace is within us all. It is our true state of being. When one person can be truly in their center, it affects thousands around them. Somewhere around 60,000 people for one person that is in their center. Inner Peace is our connection with our Divine Spark. That divine part of ourselves that, which no matter what happens to us, always remains untouched. As you realize this place within yourself, you awaken more to it. Inner peace is a state of being. A state of being that you can consciously shift into. You just contemplate inner peace and it is there. It is hard to place into words what IS. When I am there I am in utter bliss. All of these thoughts and ideas that I share with you are methods of coming to bliss in any moment. Finding bliss in any and all moments is the key to lasting happiness and true inner peace.

> "It's not what we have. It's what we believe."
> ~ 3 Doors Down in 'It's not my Time'

Inner Peace is not dependent upon the conditions that surround us. It is, however, dependent upon our perspective. As the saying goes: Be in the world, but not of it. And my favorite quote from Gandhi: "Be the change you wish to see in the world."

Be Inner Peace and you will see more of it. As you focus on that, it expands! You are the change you wish to see in the world. It is in all of us to create peace and balance on the

Earth. As we do this within our selves, first, we are affecting the frequencies of the planet. One by one we each add up in numbers causing a change in vibration for peace and harmony. Don't wait for someone else to do it anymore. It's upon each and every one of us to feel and be peace. Once we find that within us (and it is within us all) we then emanate that out to the world. We are affecting change just by being what we desire. The vibrations of the planet will be affected as we do this. We are the Mother Earth and the Mother Earth is us.

I was reminded in a workshop I attended that the grid that is a part of Mother Earth is about four feet off the ground. This means that we are not actually walking on the Earth but IN the Earth. We truly ARE of Mother Earth. So as you affect changes within you, it truly is being felt immediately throughout the Earth. As more of us do this, the frequencies of the Earth and in ourselves dramatically shift to a higher vibration. Take time to be.

Yes, it definitely can be a challenge when we see the reality of difficult situations occurring before us from the ground level. If we can just rise above while riding the wave, the force of the impact is not felt as much so the ferocity of it will not be as tumultuous. Not only that, but if you rise above and live in your inner peace you are assists in creating peace you desire in the world just be BEING peace.

For me it is a natural progression where I am becoming more aware of my conscious shift into this state of being . . . One beautiful moment at a time. These moments seem to be speeding up and lasting longer. I seem to be able to remember this state of being more and more throughout the day, and as I remember I bring it to the surface and at the same time bring myself to this state. I become One with my true inner self, my divine spark, my connection to source.

Follow the simple and comical advice heard on the Dr. Phil show: "You too can find inner peace". Dr Phil proclaimed, "The way to achieve inner peace is to finish all the things you have started and have never finished." Someone in the television audience comments on the show: "So, I looked around my house to see all the things I started and hadn't finished, and before leaving the house this morning, I finished a bottle of Merlot, a bottle of Zinfandel, a bottle of Bailey's Irish Cream, a bottle of Kailua, a package of Oreos, the remainder of my old Prozac prescription, the rest of the cheesecake, some Doritos, and a box of chocolates. You have no idea how freaking good I feel right now." ⇐ An example of where our sense of humor comes in. Humor assists us in raising our vibrations.

I'm finding more and more when I reach my Inner peace, my center, I am better able to not attach to an outcome and choose the best outcome I desire. It's a natural progression for me. And that no matter what is going on around me; I can remain in my center. My peace. As I do this, my outer surrounding naturally shift and change into this realm I am in. Whether it happens immediately or over time is not the point. It happens within you and that is what matters most.

For instance, one day I was playing with my baby Bella who, at the time, was 18-months old. I was pulling her down the hallway by her hands, as her cute pajamas were slippery and she was loving it. I didn't take into account her still fragile growing arms and must have pulled something, because she starting crying and not moving that arm. I went back and forth between wanting to take her to the hospital and waiting it out to see if it was a quick thing and she would be okay. We knew her arm wasn't broken because touching it didn't make her cry out in pain and she was still moving her fingers occasionally.

I gave her something for the pain and turned the Reiki on. I tried to squash the guilt within me that I "caused" this issue. I then had to squash the fear of needing to take her to the emergency room. Then I had to wonder if I somehow caused this for some sort of victim (ego) experience and, therefore, needing to release it once and for all. So I did some inner connecting within myself. I brought myself to a divine place, saw Bella as the beautiful whole and complete self she already is and sleeping peacefully. This was a back and forth progression where I was finally able to get into an allowing state of "what will be will be" and still with my goal and just surrendering (while still flowing with energy). She finally went to sleep an hour and a half later, slept through the night and did not complain much the next day at all. It's as if it never happened. I knew this was a major lesson for me, not her. She was just there to assist in the mirrors.

I've found that the key to what brings true inner peace for me is practicing all the varying forms of yoga. Yoga is the key ingredient for smoothing out Kundalini processes as well as assisting in getting your mind, body and soul there safely. This practice is centuries old. The ancient ones who cultivated this knew then what was and is best for our multi-dimensional selves. It is immensely beneficial and highly recommended. I'm finding my practices are very much in line with Hinduism, Buddhism and the Tao. Yoga is well-rounded and has its roots in India within Hinduism and Buddhism. It is not just simply the art of movements and poses in yoga (called asanas), as most may know of yoga. It is so much more than that. Yoga allows you to prepare your mind, body and soul through utilizing mental, physical, and spiritual disciplines of yoga. There are forms of yoga that work with meditation (i.e. yoga nidra—a form of meditation that takes you through similar stages of sleep while remaining conscious), energy, mind, breath/pranayama, movement, dedicated service, or focused contemplation on a deity or spiritual concept.

Yvonne Kason, M.D. states in her superb book *Farther Shores* of yoga's benefits and Kundalini's involvement, "With the grace of the Divine, the Kundalini/spiritual energy may then awaken in the prepared spiritual aspirant, and rise up the spine and pass through the chakras—the energy centers or vortices that exist along the spine and in the brain. When Kundalini has fully awakened it reaches the seventh chakra, located at the crown of the head, and the yogi attains Samadhi, an experience of mystical union." And there is Buddha's, "To keep the body in good health is a duty . . . otherwise we shall not be able to keep our mind strong and clear." You can cultivate a personal sadhana (practice) that is extremely powerful for your growth as a spiritual being in physical form. As you practice your form of yoga for life, you will see that there is a flow. You have the choice to resist the flow or be in the flow. You will notice as you allow and surrender to the flow of life and your practices that the natural rhythm of life comes easy and feels so much better than if you had resisted.

Sometimes you've got to reach for it. You've to go consciously reach for peace, happiness and self-realization. Once you are in it there is a flow and no more need to "try". Peace is our natural way of being but sometimes an initial effort is what gets us to open up to what already is. By this I mean there sometimes has to be some sort of initiation on your part for what you desire, especially when coming from an opposite state of being of what you desire. There is something inside of all of us that desires something better; something more; something sublime, uplifting and peaceful. Your creative expression will not come to you while you sit and eat bon bons. So you "reach" from the depths of those low vibrational states for that uplifting vibration. Another way of saying it is you start to remove the blockages that clears the way for you to see the bliss that has always been within. This "reach" is innate within us all and when it is triggered it pulls us to the Divine (and our truest selves) exponentially.

I tend to ramble on and confuse the issue sometimes. In keeping it simple: Think positive, be happy, loving and grateful consciously *all the time* and as you do this you naturally follow your true path and those experiences naturally flow to you without any effort just because you decided to be happy, loving and grateful.

The trick is to always listen to that intuitive divine voice inside of you. It doesn't always tell you things you like to hear but if you remain conscious and present you will know and feel it is right. As you are present in the Now you will always be living from the truest state of being. There's something within you that knows when you are in the right space within yourself or not. Striking signs when not in the right state of being are feeling depressed, moody and irritable. But eventually many will wake up to this feeling and strike back, reach up and live from their true divine nature. You reach by way of creating from that divine intuition that comes to you. The creation that is you is creating and expanding further.

It's like when you are physically reaching for something on a high shelf. As you stretch you will go further and further. You'll notice in yoga that you are constantly stretching, reaching and strengthening while surrendering at the same time. You extend and then surrender; extend, surrender. Expanding as the Universe is constantly evolving. Each time you do a pose (asana) you notice you can go just a little bit further; you are just a little bit stronger; just a little bit more flexible. Sometimes a helping hand is needed, so you ask for a chair (aka Shaktipat, Spiritual Counseling, Reiki, Angels, etc.). Other times the Divine offers you assistance. Where suddenly you notice a stool (aka intuitive guidance, spontaneous answer, synchronistic events, and people or situations suddenly appearing to help you). This stool allows for easier access to what you're reaching for. Finally, there are times when it is necessary for more effort on your part. You realize you really can stretch further as a natural progression. Suddenly you're there! Success!

How can we surrender and reach at the same time? I'm still working on it all. I'm not perfect, but I am sharing what has worked for me in times past. As always, take what you like and leave the rest. There is a delicate balance. Yes, we must follow our own divine/intuitive reception for expressing what is truly innate within us as a unique soul expressing the divine. For my Husband it is drumming; for me yoga with spiritual expression to assist others in finding their unique expression, staying the path and working through those challenges; for others its singing and teaching, playing the guitar, caring for children. For some it actually is emulating that peace and simply BEing peace all the time. Many of us will toggle the balance of BEing peace while expressing whatever it is that is our Divine gifts within us. I'm not quite there yet being peace all the time, but it's part of what I reach for as my path.

We contribute as a part of the whole and become one with our expressions; our truth. Whatever flows naturally is what we aim our *enthusiasm* towards—an enthusiasm for life and all it divinely drives us to do. Not necessarily "do" but be in alignment with what makes you the most happiest. So we follow that path and this may require putting beautiful positive life force energy into it. It might require more positive thinking/gratitude/love to be in the vibrational alignment for receiving such. It is unique for each of us what blockages we are to release and what we are divinely guided to Be, experience and expand upon. Just the act of trying alone is not surrendering to Source. There is a fine line between trying and naturally, intuitively reaching with enthusiasm for a more natural way of being.

My life was blah till I finally starting thinking more consciously and more consciously positive; aiming only those positive vibrations out. Surrounding myself with only those things that feel good; gaining the ability to listen to my heart finally. As we emulate this frequency out, higher vibrational experiences of the same vibration naturally flow to us. I learned from great teachers and am still learning. In becoming conscious, I was aware of negative thoughts that only kept me down. I saw my light and stretched it wider and wider. I surrender to the outcome knowing I am always in a positive enthusiastic frame of being, always allowing for the magic and surprises the Universe can bring. And by "always" I mean as much as humanly possible and I strive for it. Then, surrender allowing room for the Universe to do its 'thang'. Yes, things will still happen, as in life and while living in the higher positive vibration you are in your peace and can handle that flow better. These challenges that happen will just pass on by. You are in that flow. You are peace.

Key ingredients to true inner peace are the inner workings of acceptance, enthusiasm and enjoyment. As I analyze or rather witness my states of being throughout the day I am finding the most peace from these three states of being. Even Eckhart Tolle states in his book, *A New Earth*, that these states are the only three states of being for every moment: Enthusiasm, enjoyment and acceptance. All the rest can be cast aside. These states are key in staying in the present moment and inner peace.

Enthusiasm has been a big synchronicity for me this week and so I am taking the big hint from the Divine and sharing this with you now. Think about it, when you are in the moment of being enthusiastic about an endeavor you are about to embark upon you are in a natural high vibrational state. You're excited and blissful! Nothing can stop that beautiful energy of yours. When I am enthusiastic about something I am looking forward to the full experience of it as well. For me, I am enthusiastic about yoga and all its inner workings. And as I've already said am certified to teach Hatha Yoga and continue to learn more deeply about yoga and its inner working. I teach yoga through one health fitness club right now and aspire to work in a yoga studio in the near future as well. My enthusiasm for yoga spills into my daily life and I walk on air. This is just like being enthusiastic about a passion of yours. Again for me it's the passion to show others they can be happy in life and follow their bliss. This is my passion so I come off as enthusiastic while talking to others about this. I light up inside and this light beams out to others. What is my bliss or enthusiasm is what comes naturally to me and this is the same for each and every one of you.

Likewise, when you are simply moving through enjoyment the feeling is contagious and you are simply being and sharing in the present moment. Enjoyment is in the midst of a beautiful summer day at the beach, it's holding your baby girl in your arms and flying her in the air, it's the smell of flowers on a beautiful spring day, it's the bliss from drumming your heart out on your favorite drums, it's the new song that suddenly comes on the radio that excites, it's the excited chatter with friends, it's the delight of ice-cream in the middle of summer, it's the thrill of riding in go-carts while hearing your child's' exuberant laughter, it's the simple pleasure of being in the present moment no matter where you are. You get the idea. Enthusiasm is the excitement of a positive outcome no matter the circumstances. Being in a positive frame of mind such as enthusiasm for positive occurrences brings about positive experiences because it is a high vibration. When you are in that higher vibration you naturally attract that which you are!

And here comes acceptance. Yes, this one is one that can be a challenge to reach at times. Because there are times when you've reach a negative snag in the road and you don't want to accept or surrender to the situation at hand. However, you eventually have to get to that point in order to move beyond the rough experience you may be going through. If you don't, you are in a form of resistance and the issue will only get worse until you accept that it exists and allow it to be in your space for a time while you shed the processed learning's from it. But once you accept the situation as is, even in the midst of the strife, you are in connection with Source. You've tapped in and said, "Okay, I'll accept this. I know it has to be here right now. I'll see what lessons it holds for me and know that everything happens for a reason. It's okay. This too shall pass." Once you've accepted and surrendered to the situation, you're already beyond it. Magic happens and it's suddenly seemingly fixed itself. Amazing!

And when this happens you're back to enjoyment! Enjoying the positive changes that have occurred and living in the present moment. Soon you may find something to be enthusiastic about again, a new workshop, job, friend, partner, song, pet, child, sunny day, healthy day, and so on! Observe your state right now. Ask yourself, "Which of these three am I feeling?" If it is not one of these three, ask yourself why. Ask what needs to be released in order for you to move into these higher states of being. These states of being are ones to strive for in every moment. Enthusiasm, acceptance and enjoyment are key components to true inner peace.

So using the stretching analogy, you will also notice your enthusiasm drives your stretch for what you are reaching for. Acceptance may be necessary for the present moment in just surrendering to continue to reaching right now. As you accept you relax into the stretch. Other times you are content in enjoying the stretch (aka the ride or the climb of life if you will). You simply breathe out ahhhhh as you stretch and enjoy. The benefits are noticed along the way and gratitude comes naturally.

I have to say that my connection to God is truly my highest peace in all situations. No matter what is happening or what is going on in life, I always have the Divine/God/Universe. When I remember and connect to this, it is the ultimate release of tension, stress, worry and fear. It is the ultimate feeling of peace. This connection is a knowing that the Almighty Divine is All That Is and nothing can ever take that from me, as it IS me. It is ever constant! We are One. We are ALL One with the Divine. Connect to that knowing and you are in bliss.

To follow, I share more of what has brought me true inner peace. These can act as guide posts along your way to True Inner Peace, Kundalini awakening and Self-realization. Peace is our constant. Our soul is always at peace. And we can bring that to our waking consciousness, either in little steps or a leap. It is up to you. And it is my intention that this will assist you in getting there.

Chapter 10

Find Your Balance

Balance is key. In these times, it's so easy to overdo it because of what you notice in your outer world. That reality does not have to be yours, unless you believe it does. You will get whatever it is you believe. When you have a belief, you attract all experiences that will confirm your belief. This is Universal Law. Whether it is a negative belief or a positive belief, you will attract it. So it is helpful to get to the core of your beliefs and be sure you are attracting what you truly want and not what some very old belief that is not serving you brings to you.

For example, you have a goal and it's a great goal too. You want so much for it to be done. However, are you enjoying the ride while it happens? Are you reaching for this goal a bit too hard? I am not about the destination so much anymore but rather the Journey. It's all about enjoying the here and now because that's all we have.

I heard an example from, I believe, Abraham-Hicks that says it best. There is a man who works long hours to achieve a goal of completing a project (and, who knows, maybe get promoted). He works "to the bone", barely sleeps, is grumpy with his friends and family more than usual. It takes him a year, maybe two, to reach his goals. He's finally there. But what did he give up? He gave up his free time. He gave up his well-being. He gave up feeling good along the way. We must enjoy the ride.

What did this man just manifest by the Universal Law of Attraction? He just attracted more experiences that will attract this same feeling he has been feeling during the past year or two while reaching his goal. He attracted more exhaustion, more projects that require long hours, more time away from family and friends and most importantly his well-being. His soul is suffering. Balance is the key.

In the wise words of Abraham-Hicks, "You can never have a happy ending at the end of an unhappy journey; it just doesn't work out that way. The way you're feeling, along the way, is the way you're continuing to pre-pave your journey, and it's the way it's going to continue to turn out until you do something about the way you are feeling."

Another example: I have a goal for my new web site design. However, I have a day job, a part-time job in the Spiritual Realm, a family and the requirement for balance in my life. So in the right time I will achieve my new web design goals, but I will not suffer in the process. I will not give up the sleep my body requires or the exercise and walks it needs to rejuvenate. I will not give up my wonderful family time. So I will balance my daily work responsibilities with my family and free time. And when there is time the web design happens naturally. It somehow works out perfectly and I am in balance.

"Yes, there are many things that need to get done, but in this moment I have to do nothing." ~ Oprah Winfrey

Now back to the example of the hard working man who gave up his soul to get a project done. There must be a core belief somewhere in his being that told him in order to be happy he must work, or in order to make money he must work hard and suffer along the way, or there could be any number of reasons why this man is working hard. But to figure that out, it's an individual process. He himself must work on finding those answers within him, as he is the only one who truly knows. He can work with a spiritual hypnotherapist if he chooses or start with working by himself. Again, it's an individual process and no way is wrong.

EXERCISE:

Try this inner dialogue with yourself every day. Start now. Ask yourself questions in every moment for every thought and especially when you receive an experience that is not pleasing to you. This may or may not be serving your highest good. So for the highest good, you will ask to rid yourself of the core beliefs that attracted this situation. Ask your Angels for guidance and assistance in ridding yourself of old negative beliefs. You will notice patterns that will assist you in figuring out what you are attracting. I dive deeper into core beliefs in Book Two: *Divine Embrace.*

Take a few moments in privacy and meditation to dig deeper into yourself. The idea here is to rid yourself of more of your ego. To peel another layer off and find the true 100% perfect, whole, and complete self you already are. In meditation or in a space where you will not be interrupted start the questioning process.

If you have a specific experience in mind, hold that experience in your mind as you ask. Ask yourself: **"What must I believe in order for this experience to exist in my reality?"** Don't dig for the answer. It will just come to you.

Then ask yourself to go deeper. As you get deeper into the questions you may come up with a surface belief. Don't stop there. Only stop when you really feel it in your core. You may even feel a twinge in your solar plexus or deep in your belly. Go as far as you can and ask for this belief that no longer serves you to be removed.

Then ask that the Angels and the Divine/God/Goddess to fill this (now hole) with pure Divine light. Visualize pure white light filling you up and rejuvenating you for a fresh start. Pure intention is enough and will flow through you.

I wish you a balanced life always!

Chapter 11

Mind Awareness

"I am aligned with the Universe,
and the Universe is aligned with me.
No longer my mind,
I am free." ~ Maggie Anderson

I couldn't believe it. I did it again! I totally and completely identified with my mind. Oh there were bouts of bliss, of that connectedness to the One Source, but I was back in. I was in the illusion in a major way! The ups, the downs, the yin, the yang.

It took receiving a link from a friend of an article by the wonderful Eckhart Tolle to remind me (*You Are Not Your Mind* blog post). And I thank you very deeply! I had already read his books "The Power of Now" and "A New Earth." And so I read again what I had known before and soaked it up like it was new . . . because it was, all over again.

I wrote this excerpt for this book when in the blissful connected moments we all bounce in and out of till we reach total consciousness. We will all get there and then we will "know." Mind thoughts are a disease that most all of us are afflicted and must rid ourselves of. It is time to be the witness and be free from the disease. Free from our thoughts to simply BE!

Our suffering is rooted at the conditionings of the mind and not really the circumstances of our lives. Outer circumstances when accepted and no longer denied or judged are simply that; just circumstances for us to work through in life. But the conditionings of our minds cause unhappiness because it starts to judge circumstances, deny them, ridicule them, get impatient with them and basically is unwilling to allow it to be there in the present moment and accept it for its beingness. The mind thought says it "shouldn't" be there so our suffering begins. But when we accept it and allow it to be there, the challenge transmutes into a better flowing experience. Peace occurs in that very moment and that allows for the challenge to be handled more efficiently. It tends to be worked through more expediently.

Be still. Become the witness. Rid yourself of nonsense thoughts. Get rid of negative thoughts about self, about others, about life, and about pretty much everything. The space between is where you can feel utter bliss. Let go of all thought and just be. Try to observe the space between your thoughts, the space between someone else's thoughts, the space between a musical note, and the space between anything. Here you find true connection with the Divine. As Osho gracefully states, "When the mind is silent you are in communion with existence; when the mind is noisy you are disconnected. Your own noise functions like a wall around you. Silence is the bridge."

Now, also, positive thoughts bring about positive experiences. The more positive you are the better you feel from within. You can start there. Simply monitor your thoughts. Just watch them without judgment. What are you thinking and feeling now? Right now? Release it. It is not you. It is only the ego that you identify with, but it is not the real you.

Feel the love and gratitude for all you have in your life in this very moment. As you do this you align with higher vibrations that are speeding their way to you with positive experiences.

You truly are doing awesome. We must remember, as much as possible, not to get down on ourselves. When we get down on ourselves, we are talking negatively to our Spirit and body. We have negative thoughts and emotions. This brings our energy down and keeps it down in our energy bodies. If you are clairvoyant you can actually see the cloud of ooze and icky energy within our Energy Bodies. Bring your energy back up. Remain focused! Live in your Joy!

Simply being in the witness state allows you to move through some pretty tough times and some pretty tough ascension symptoms (ascension symptoms are mentioned at length in Book 2: *Divine Embrace*). No matter what the symptom or experience, just be with it. Let it flow through you. As you watch, as only the observer, you shine the light on the symptom or negative experience and suddenly in its right time if fades away naturally. This is life in the flow. Instead, if you resisted, the symptoms or experience would last longer and be tougher on you. In the witness state you are surrendering and allowing what will be to be, while living in the present moment.

Being the witness is explained well by Eckhart Tolle in his book *A New Earth*, "The primary cause of unhappiness is never the situation but your thoughts about it. Be aware of the thoughts you are thinking. Separate them from the situation, which is always neutral, which always is as it is. There is the situation or the fact, and here are my thoughts about it. Rather than being your thoughts and emotions, be the awareness behind them. Don't seek happiness. If you seek it, you won't find it, because seeking is the antithesis of happiness. Happiness is ever elusive, but freedom from unhappiness is attainable now, by facing what is rather than making up stories about it. Unhappiness covers up your natural state of well-being and inner peace, the source of true happiness."

An analogy in yoga comes to mind here. When you are in a pose and simply surrendering yourself to be wherever your body is in that moment for that pose, you allow the wisdom of the body to flow through. If you, however, had resisted the pose or forced yourself further into a pose that your body was not ready for, a tougher experience arises. Simply breathe and allow whatever IS in the moment. An advanced yogi or yogini is not necessarily someone who is able to do all the toughest poses at the twistiest furthest level, but instead knowing and listening to the wisdom of the body for every moment. For example, if you can do a full forward bend, excellent. If you feel you are not up for it today or not ready for a full forward bend, but go halfway, excellent! It is the wisdom of listening to that which your body tells you in every moment that teaches you the art of surrender and living in bliss now.

And remember, our thoughts are things. We create from our thoughts and emotions. We also send negative beams of energy or positive beams of energy for whoever is in our thoughts in whatever fashion they are in our thoughts. So if we are thinking not-so-nice thoughts about someone else, they are receiving that icky energy. But if we are thinking nice thoughts about someone, they are, again receiving those nice thought-energy-forms. The important thing to also know is that these thoughts/emotions/ energy we create within ourselves always comes back to us multiplied. We think something it comes back to us much larger. So the more you see positive things and think positive things, the more you receive those. The same goes for the negative energy.

It's important to also know that all things in our outer reality is a mirror reflected back to us what is INSIDE of US! So whatever you are seeing, whatever you are noticing, whatever you are judging, whatever you are critiquing is ALL YOU. Whatever you see is something inside you that you created. So it's very helpful to always see the best in people and the best in all situations. As you do this you create energy multiplied in those positive stances you take.

Meditation is a perfect way to become aware of your thoughts and to rid yourself of those nasty useless things.

In meditation you can easily become centered and still. We have useful logical thinking that proves helpful for day-to-day things, but outside of this our thoughts are mostly negative or not necessary. Try a meditation where you actually listen for the space between. It's the space between that carries beauty and grace. The more you practice this, the easier it becomes and the more aware and blissful you become (or rather bring back to the surface of who you truly are). Just breathe. Relax. And be.

Our mind thoughts are a disease. Thinking is a disease and since most all of us have this thinking disease we don't know it's a disease. Thinking is a part of the illusion we must remove in order to feel the Oneness with Self and with the All That Is. Our thinking keeps us in the drama and illusions of life. Our thinking causes the suffering we incur every day. We can separate ourselves from the thinking mind and remember we are not separate from others or the world around us. We ARE all One.

Our thoughts create emotions. And sometimes our thoughts seemingly conflict with our emotions. However, that is because we are not aware of our deeply unconscious thoughts from our past selves in this life and others. Become the witness of the emotions instead. That is the core of the truth to witness. There you will simply observe without judgment and then giggle with freedom from ever needing to be in the illusion again! So here is your reminder once again. Remember to be the witness. Remember to simply Be. In that space you are connected and you are Bliss.

"In music, a grace note is the pause between notes that is so important to the pacing of a song. Grace is the state we are in when we are doing nothing but just being who we are."
~ Madisyn Taylor, Daily OM

Chapter 12

The Presence is On

Present Moment

Take a moment to ask yourself, "What is your awareness in this very moment?" Breathe deeply and listen. The calm that overcomes you is the stillness of the Divine.

Being in the present moment means living only in the *right Now*. Right in this very moment, how do you feel? Are you happy? Are you content? Are you relaxed? What are you thinking? Any number of things will come up. However, if any of those things are worry or fear about the past or worry and fear about some future event, then you are *not* in the present moment. If you are feeling worry or fear you are not grounded and are not in the present moment. If you take a look at your very present moment, more than likely you will notice that you are doing just fine. You are happy; you are reading this after all!

You are safe and content in most moments. As you live more in the present moment you start to realize the blessings within you and around you in every moment and you realize these moments are more and more in your life than had you not taken the time to focus and live in the present moment!

You will be amazed at some of the thoughts you will catch yourself thinking as you coming into the present moment. A friend of mine who is very positive on the outside was shocked to find out how negative her thoughts were at herself when she went on a silent retreat (no talking is aloud at a silent retreat). This is a tremendous epiphany that truly assists one to realize their thoughts are wreaking havoc in their system. Take an hour or a day or in every moment you can remember and watch your thoughts. How negative are you thoughts to yourself compared to what you would say to a loved one. Would you call a loved one an idiot? No, but I bet you might catch your thoughts telling yourself that. It's all relative of course. But if these thoughts are affecting you negatively—which usually they are on a deep level—then you need to wake up to them. You need to change your thoughts to your SELF first. Being present allows you the awareness to live in gratitude and bliss and there is no room for negative self talk anymore. Take notice and be present Now.

The present moment may mean coming to terms with what you are feeling now, which may not be all positive and hunky dory. However, that is perfect and healthy! Admit it to yourself in the very moment. It is healing to go through your emotions immediately as you are feeling them. Rather than allowing them to be buried or fester over them for far too long. Buried emotions will fester in the body and become stronger and harder to deal with later. If you allow yourself the time to feel the emotions, to cry or to be upset and truly process the emotion in the moment, then further aggravated symptoms will not manifest themselves. Coming to terms with whatever is in the present moment is astoundingly transforming. Once you accept what is, no matter the circumstance, it can then be released. You've shined your light on the challenge and realize it is just that, another circumstance to realize your peace lies within. You can then create something new from whatever challenge is occurring now by accepting it, not repressing it. Create from the Now.

For example, someone who overeats may be burying emotional or stressful feelings with food instead of being present with the emotions or admitting they are stressed out. This is how I used to process on my tougher days and part of the reasons for the weight I had gained. An overeater is usually someone who's used food as a way to cope with tough situations, stress and emotional issues. You can usually see this physically by the extra weight if using this coping mechanism over time. Whereas you might not immediately notice in someone else who buries emotions with other addictions (such as alcoholism, work-a-holic, etc.) But these, too, will manifest physical symptoms eventually if not dealt with and brought to the present moment to process the issues that have been buried.

So if you stop the cookie before it gets to your mouth and ask yourself if you are hungry, you will realize you probably are not hungry. Then ask yourself what you are really feeling right now. You may realize you are thinking about something that makes you sad or upset, i.e. an event or person. Or you are stressed from all the things you need to do or haven't done yet. Once you admit to these emotions and feelings you start to process them **in the present moment** rather than burying them with food. Then you start to Be in the present moment and after the healthy processing time passes you are again in a healthy present state of mind, simply feeling good.

As you go through the challenging emotions in the present moment, they subside much more quickly and much more easily. Remember that saying: Hear the whispers or you will hear the screams. You'll even find some transformational occurrences when in physical pain and moving through that pain while living in the present moment. You'll find the pain goes away faster. You'll find more epiphanies regarding why the pain is there and what your evolution from that incident will be going forward.

However, there is being in the present moment and having a future worry that you've already done all you can do to alleviate that stress or worry. For example, let's say there is a money issue. Let's say you are on the verge of foreclosing on your home and you've worked with the bank and tried all you can do. You are hoping to sell the home in order to alleviate foreclosure proceedings. In the mean time, what do you do? Worry? Hope someone buys your house. Sure! But beyond making the wish for the best, affirming: "Money flows easily and effortlessly to you now from all directions", calling in the Divine for extra assistance and thinking positive, processing the stressful moments that come up, the thing to do is to stop worrying. Stop worrying about the "What If's" that keep coming into your MIND. Your ego loves the drama and the negative thoughts that keep it alive. Stop worrying about the future. Start being present right now. Right now you are healthy and happy and enjoying time with the kids, thriving at a job, the list goes on. Think of the RIGHT NOW present positives in your life. And feel presently that all truly is well.

As you get out of the worry and fear of the future and the past, you move into the present moment. The present moment rocks! It holds blissful states of being and powerful transformations. It helps you realize that those 3D reality experiences are simply just that, experiences. You can add it to your resume when you cross over to the Other Side. But you will gain much in "points" if you can live in the present blissful moment and still process current lower reality experiences. But remember to simply process them as they come and not allow them to boil, not allow the ego to wallow for too long. Simply healthily process and let it go.

Being in the present moment allows you to move through many of the things I mention in this book and many healing transformations. Powerful results occur at such a high speed when in the present moment. Such as: surrendering, allowing, more easily releasing emotions and feelings, bringing gratitude to your state of being naturally, and my favorite feeling bliss!

I was at my sister's graduation/wedding celebration recently and experienced a blissful moment that seemed to stretch on forever. All of our family and friends were there. People laughing, talking, enjoying and living. My Husband had finished a beautiful jam session drumming with the family and my nephew, Ryan, on guitar. And for this moment my Husband was in his element cooking at the grill and me behind him on the deck. I looked over to my daughter who was blissfully blowing bubbles with the other kids. Bubbles were everywhere. The song *Everything,* an Alanis Morisette song, came on the radio at that moment. And I stopped. I looked around slowly. I knew I was smiling. I felt an amazing connection with everyone and also with the happiness of the moment. Bubbles were mystically floating in the air. Beautiful scents of flowers and grilled food filled the air. Lots of laughter! It seemed to go by in slow motion as I enjoyed every drop of this moment. I wanted to stop and point it out to someone, anyone. But instead I remained in this state for as long as it lasted.

These blissful moments can happen at any time any where. They can be from a happy moment or a sorrow-filled moment. They can come through the darkness into the light and suddenly you see the present moment for what is always was and is. All moments are Divine.

By being present and in a blissful state you are also in an allowing state of being. You are allowing the Universe to fully support you. You will see how fully supported you really are, simply by being fully in the present moment and enjoying each moment as the Now. Your blissful state of existence opens you up to higher vibrations and higher experiences and vibrationally aligned people are naturally propelled in your direction. These same benefits come from a peaceful meditating state of mind. When you are meditating you are relaxed and present.

Grounding is an excellent exercise to get you into the present moment if you feel you have gone out of living in the Now. Go to the *Stand in the Earth—Grounding* chapter in this book to practice the many grounding exercises available. In conscious awareness of the present moment, love flows into all you do more fluidly and naturally. Simply breathe; be aware of your present moment now.

Chapter 13

Meditation—Go Within

Through meditation you can access the inner realms of the divine soul. Go within. Meditation is a master **key** component of a daily devoted practice that I strongly recommend. Meditation is a subtle yet powerful force that allows you to come back to yourself. To really see your True Self again.

The activity of our lives may take us out of our center and out of being in our knowing of the Self. Meditation gives us the breathing space to come back to our knowing. I would like to emphasize how important meditation is to your spiritual growth and well-being. Not only that, but many of us now know the powerful benefits of relaxations techniques that truly reduce physical symptoms from stress. We also have the striking benefits of released endorphins and other chemicals in the brain that naturally occur during meditation. Meditation washes away the darkness of our minds and shines the light paving the way for peace. Meditation allows us to see things as they truly are to the core of the Universe. As we slow down and still our mind we suddenly see the truth and do not get caught up in 3D illusions. We open up to full clarity of the present moment without the fears of from past or the future. Our ego's and personality dissolve, as our authentic Divine self emerges. Meditation is a subtle but powerful way to become closer with our Higher Self, Angels, Guides, God and basically in getting to know your true self once again. We are being guided. We have been guided all our life. And now you and I are being guided to get to know that which has guided us, which is truly your Self. Your higher self if you will. Meditation is the means to Self-Realization and Inner Peace.

I recommended practicing meditation daily at a consistent set time to be with yourself. Early morning or later in the evenings are great times to meditate as there is more stillness in the air from the frenzy of activity that happens during the day. Less energy from mass consciousness is berating your system. An hour would be nice, but if you can afford 5-15 minutes that will be a great beginning. As you do this you gain momentum as well as the many benefits of meditation. Although to begin, it is a great practice to have a set time. Joseph Campbell reminds us that our spirit needs time daily, "You must have a room, or a certain hour or so a day, where you don't know what was in the newspaper that morning, you don't know who your friends are, you don't know what you owe anybody, you don't know what anybody owes you. This is a place where you can simple experience and bring forth what you are and what you might be."

And one of the several beautiful benefits is to the brain! Like Kim Marcille Romaner explains in her book, *The Science of Making Things Happen,* "The Tibetan Dalai Lama has participated in brain research since the 1990s, dispatching some of his most experienced practitioners to the United States for testing. Researchers discovered that the monks' brains behave differently than the brains of those who do not meditate. Gamma waves moving through the monks' brains were more powerful, as were waves associated with perception, problem solving, and consciousness. The longer a monk had been practicing, the more pronounced the change in the brain".

Eventually, you will notice the meditative state of mind is flowing with you always. It's the stillness within. This state is a rising of consciousness and awareness to your Divine self. To have this state in most moments of your day assists you in staying in the Divine flow of life. To really listen and be aware of what is happening around you while remaining in your center to flow with life rather than be separate from it. This is what I have found and experienced in my daily meditation practice. You take it with you wherever you go. I have found utter bliss and the highest love when meditating and from the effects of meditating. You come in touch with the Divine aka your true self here. You can take this feeling and connection with you in your daily life.

All of the answers are within you. There is no need to ask of another. However, it is sometimes helpful to hear another speak or hear of their experience in order to go within and find the answers or ah-ha moments for yourself. We have an inner compass for life. When we check in with our divine self, the answers are immediately there. As you follow your true inner guidance the flow in your life is smooth, no matter the circumstance. But if you second guess yourself and go against your gut feelings from within, more challenges than you need to face may arise. The road may get bumpier than need-be. So go within, feel at the very core your true essence. Your soul never lies. You will feel good about the right path and not-so-great about a less-than-smooth path.

Although there may be questions, be open to the mystery. Allow the mystery to be there and enjoy it as it unfolds. In meditation this deeper allowing state is reached. Because in your soul you know, no matter what is happening, at the very core is peace and tranquility. In being open to the mystery you are also open to more magic and miracles to naturally occur in your life every day. In meditation you accept what is and no longer force a situation to change but see the lessons in them and move through situations. Matt Kahn of TrueDivineNature. com notes in his video that in trying to change what is, you are perpetuating your own suffering. You may be resisting by trying to change something in your life. Matt Kahn states further to stop resisting and come to a place of love for whatever is happening in your life. You will come to a place of loving the one that life is happening to. The only constant is change. This realization may be a peaceful concept to you that allows you to open up to the wonders of the world! A beautiful saying for this is: This too shall pass.

A relaxed state of mind shows the Universe that you are open and allowing what will be to be. As you are relaxed the Universe feels this by Law of Attraction and immediately rushes to your side and brings you all that you desire to manifest and more in supporting you completely. Meditation can assist us in aligning with our true deepest self and therefore move away from surface ego desires. This assists with the Law of Attraction working for our highest benefit. The meditative state of mind aligns with the true self. We no longer activate the law of attraction for those surface ego agendas. But rather we get out of our surface ego desires and into our hearts and allow the Law of Attraction to bring us the true alignment of our highest wellbeing. You will find the Law of Attraction working better for you in this state.

In this state, your walls come down and only bliss remains. As you meditate more consistently this feeling comes to you naturally. And there comes a time where meditating comes so easily you may not have to meditate for a half hour or an hour in order to reach a relaxed, open, blissful state of being. This feeling will simply be with you always.

In conjunction with meditating daily, take time out daily for solitude. Time for yourself to just Be—whether that is walking in nature, sitting in your living room reading or feeling the peace of the moment. You can decide to remove all the distractions, noise and mind thoughts that are in your way. Just wash them away and start in a clean fresh state. Take a deep breath and feel renewed. Of course, the challenges that come up in your life are your red flags to pay attention to something that you are missing. So it's it not that you wash away something unpleasant, but that you see it and recognize it for what it is. So in meditation you are able to process it and see the deeper meaning behind why this is occurring or what you feel drawn to possibly do or not do next in order to come back to a balanced state of being for yourself. Do this in any moment you feel more stress than usual. Do this countless times a day for connecting back to your true self again. Bring meditation into your daily living as your constant way of being.

Samskara's are deeply stored imprints from actions and desires asleep in the unconscious. During meditation and Kundalini releases samskara's can be released without ever becoming active. (Kundalini and Samskara's are discussed further in Book Two: *Divine Embrace*.) Once they are active, they produce the desires and result in actions creating more karma. So here you know the goal is to not accumulate more karma but to release those unconscious actions and desires before they become active and to stay in a neutral non-dual state of being. Meditation is one key element that will assist in release samskara's. Some things that occur to let you know that samskara's are being released are visions or images, hearing voices, memories, symbols and emotions. These types of things occur commonly during meditation and also during Kundalini releases. There is no need to focus on these, but to allow them to flow through you and release. Your state of awareness has filters that determine how you perceive everything. Every expectation, preconceived notion, every thought puts a filter into your clarity of awareness. So you perceive through a filter. Most all of us have filters. Through meditation, Kundalini awakenings and spiritual work we are able to dissolve the filters and ego personality while integrating our higher selves and opening up to who we truly are and always have been: our Divine Essence. As you naturally flow, samskara's are gone and you are more able to obtain and remain in the state of Oneness. As you can see, the benefits of meditation go to the core of our essence!

Meditation will allow you to surrender to what's happening right here in the very present moment. We only have right now and in practicing meditation you come to the awareness that it is okay that whatever is happening is happening. Because whatever it happening is happening for a reason to bring our attention to it and resolve those patterns within ourselves. So while a challenge is occurring we can be in the moment and surrender to the fact that it is happening. And from that presence we can work our way through the issues because we are open to its existence and clarity of mind and soul combined brings awareness to what we can then do or not do to bring ourselves back to peaceful alignment with wellbeing.

Meditation will allow you to feel the awareness of the Now; to eventually live only within present moment. Because our reality truly is only what's happening right now, not in the future or the past. So this awareness is our true reality. What a load off that is! No more worrying about the future. No more regrets of the past. No more ego thoughts bombarding us with guilt, worry, fear, or any other thoughts forms that just don't serve us anymore. Phew! It is very freeing to know that we only have and feel what is right now. RIGHT NOW. What do you feel right now. Now is all there is. Breathe into this awareness.

There are a variety of meditation techniques out there. You can use guided meditation or nothing at all. You can sit in the quiet darkness or not. You can light a candle, incense and have soft soothing music (preferably no words, since the words will distract you). You can even do movement meditation (one of my favorites). You do not have to do any of these things or you can do them all. You have to do what feels comfortable to you. So take what you like and leave the rest. Just take time to simply Be for a while during your day.

In meditation it's a common practice to visualize a scene. Visualizing is just like daydreaming, fantasizing, etc. Have you ever played back a past event that happened and maybe even changed what actually happened in your mind? Or have you ever tried to "see" how things will go in a future event, like a date, or a baseball game, etc.? Have you ever wanted so much to tell someone off, and "daydreamed" that you were doing just that. You are seeing yourself in your "minds eye" doing this. You are using your "minds eye" to create this daydream or fantasy. It's as simple as that.

Now do not look too much into this. Don't analyze this to death. Just let the images, feeling or impressions 'come' to you. By looking too hard into this process you are creating a block in itself. What's easiest, in the beginning, is if you have visualization and/or guided meditation on CD. Someone to walk you through a meditation process will allow you to simply Be there and bliss out. You can listen to the visualization and see what is explained without having to remember anything. You can even record your own voice on tape to make your meditations that much more deep and relaxed. Then create your own details for the meditation, make it YOUR OWN. This will expand your mind. Help it flow with new images that come to you without you making it happen. Then eventually, you won't need to use the CD. The stillness within is all that will speak to you. You will also come to a place (if you haven't already) that you can obtain a sense of inner peace and wellbeing without requiring more than just your breath and conscious decision to be in your Inner Peace, your true divine soul self.

You will start to also become more aware of your surroundings. As you open up fully to the present moment through meditation. You become aware of all that is happening around you. The good and the bad. You will receive feelings about certain things and follow your gut. Divine guidance is found here. It pulls you on your path. You are naturally following the divine when in this beautiful state of being. As you become awakened and more aware, things of light will become brighter to you, and darkness even darker. Your surroundings are stronger and more in-your-face, so to speak. So always stick with your intuition on all aspects of your life. This is your guide to heading in the right direction on YOUR path. The more you meditate the higher your vibration will become and the less lower vibrational energies will be attracted to you.

"Meditation aids our conscious reconnection to source, and provides a clear channel for all our senses. Using crystals also helps to raise our vibrations, re-weaving our own crystalline matrixes with Earth energies thus decreasing our physical symptoms. Seeking the help of healers can sometimes be necessary to help us make shifts or facilitate change. Reiki, crystals, vibrational essences, DNA Light Code Activations, etc. may all be of help. Ask Spirit to guide you to someone for help with your healing." ~ Universal Life Tools

Starting to Meditate Basics

To start: Ground yourself! Picture yourself as a Tree. Or visualize cords from your feet going to the center of the Earth and a white light bursting from Earth's crystal core all the way back up the cords and into your feet, through your body and out your head. Grounding you to Mother Earth and connecting you to the Universe.

Then surround white light around you for protection. This sets the stage for a higher vibration so that you will not be susceptible to lower vibrational energies. Just picture a beautiful white light from within grow and grow to totally encompass you and your aura. Like a huge bubble or a cocoon. Feel unconditional love from the Universe to the depths of your whole being. Say your invocation of protection (this gets you into a higher vibrational state where you will not be susceptible to lower vibrations, they simply will not see you), for example:

"I invoke the Light of the Spirit here within,
I am a Clear and Perfect Channel, I am Love, I am Light."
Say this three times!

Start by getting comfortable. Take your choice of sitting up in a chair (something I tend to HAVE to do so I don't fall asleep) or against a wall cross-legged, lying down (if you can stay awake) or if you can do this comfortably sit in lotus position. Close your eyes and clear your mind (deep breath, exhale slowly) . . . don't try, just stop thinking; as you let go of your thoughts and concerns, feel yourself sinking deep into emptiness. Breathe deeply at first, in through the nose, out through the mouth. Positive IN, negative OUT. Just relax and breathe. Picture and FEEL your body relaxing, from every body part, from your feet to your head. Slowly relaxing. Your breathing should be steady. Feel your body melt and your mind float freely. Slowly but surely getting into that meditative "state", otherwise called the Alpha State. You are in a neutral place, where there should be no attachment to emotions, people, places or things. This process should be slow and usually takes no more than 10 minutes to feel the full effect. At this time you can take a few moments to tilt your head up, with your eyes closed move your eyes up to look at your third eye (in the middle of your two eye brows at the center of your forehead). Take a little time and feel the pleasant pulsation or pressure from this action. As you do this you awaken your third eye for stronger more open connections.

It's important to get into this meditative state to receive a truly neutral message. At first it may be difficult to remain neutral for questions that do pertain to you or someone close to you, but with time you can do it. The more emotional attachment we have to the person or outcome the harder it is to receive accurate information. If receiving a message is not your goal simply go with the same process and just BE in this beautiful awareness of peace and tranquility.

A thought may come in, just say "cancel" or "go away" and breathe. Then your breathing will be short and hardly noticeable. If you can half sit (like leaning on a bedpost or wall with a pillow comfortably), half lay down, that's a good position. Now some people, like me in the beginning, like to have visualizations for meditation. Like a guided meditation on a CD. I have one that I offer through my website and hope to record more soon. This book comes with another guided chakra balancing meditation that you can use alone or in conjunction with the sacred activation ceremony I entail further in this book. This can help in the beginning. If you want to receive messages you may need more time after the guided visualization just to sit and receive.

Sacred Space

You can create a sacred place where you are always safe to go, restore and connect. This place is your personal safe place to come relax, rejuvenate and heal. It is your inner realm sanctuary. Take time to make it feel and be your own. You may desire it to be a starry space field where you float and relax. Or you may desire a beach setting. My favorite is one of grassy fields, green trees sporadically placed, beautiful white and pink cherry blossom trees, flowers of all colors, with birds, butterflies, kitties and any other animals that come to me during meditation. Here in my sanctuary I come to a beautiful stream where as I was leads to a healing hot spring. I take a dip when I need cleansing and purification. Sometimes there are pools of healing waters of all the colors of the rainbow. I can simply sit and enjoy the sun-filled day. Sometimes my space is dawn or dusk and this takes me into new realms of peace. Make it your own. You may desire someone leading you in to this meditation or taping yourself to get you there without effort. This is something I offer as a Soul Journey for my clients. It is truly powerful and transformational.

Here you can meet your guides or ask to see if you can meet someone else, anyone. What happens here is real. It's not your imagination. Make it your own place. Sometimes the person you want to be there will not come, or will not come right away. Give it time and talk to whomever does actually show up to talk with you. Again asking that only the highest and best, good are aloud to come. Your Guides and Angels are there always to protect you. This may seem almost like your imagination, but it is not, it is real. Again, what happens in this place is real. The more you do this, the more real it becomes. The focus becomes clearer, you can see and hear more and receive longer clearer messages from your spirit guides and/or other beings that come into the picture.

Zen Method

Another meditation method was shown to me by a Zen Master at the Providence Zen Center in Cumberland, Rhode Island during a one day retreat. This retreat was a six hour Zen meditation. This was the longest meditation I've experienced in one sitting. We would sit in the lotus position or with legs crossed for 20 minutes in meditation and then do a walking meditation for 10-20 minutes. Then sit for 20 minutes and do a walking meditation for 10-20 minutes. And the cycle continued until complete. At sporadic times during the sitting meditation the meditation leader would walk around with a stick and ask that you lower your head to the floor exposing your back if you would like to receive a tap on your back. It is the idea that this will adjust your mind when needed as well as your body to stay present during the meditation. I'm sure there are other subtle benefits as well.

A short time in to the meditation we started to take turns going in to the Zen Master to have a discussion with him or to simply sit with him for however long we felt necessary. Some folks had long debates about spiritual or life issues. Others chose not to go in. When I went in it was about three hours into the meditation. All the questions I had thought I might ask the Zen Master went away. I no longer required answers. So I didn't have much to talk about. He gave me a great meditation tip to keep me going through the last half. He said to simply chant a mantra in my mind coordinated with my breath. Breathe in, "Don't Know"; Breathe out, "Don't Mind". Don't know, don't mind, don't know, don't mind, don't know, don't mind. This is a wise mantra. The more I learn the more I realize I know nothing. The Divine is all-knowing. So leave it up to the Divine. Freedom. Not caring about what's going on around you is more of a way of accepting what is going on as Divine. You are simply observing in a neutral but peaceful place of being. Don't know. Don't mind.

Stay Strong

If you get out of your meditation practice, don't worry about it. Worrying will only hinder your growth in meditation. This will take away the whole point of meditating. So just get back into meditating when you can. But once starting back again with it, it's like starting all over (for some). You have to get back into that "state" again. But at first, don't worry if you can't get there just yet. You will meditate and nothing spectacular may happen, no visions, no sparks. Just work back at filtering out your thoughts. Once you get back into a regular schedule, or at least doing it more often, you can finally filter your thoughts out. Then you will get better with your intuition and your goals on strengthening your connection. But worrying about meditating and making contact you're your higher Source right away is not going to help you get there faster, it will only hinder you.

Meditation is the discipline of clearing the mind to explore your inner self. In the meditative state, one has almost completely shut out the outside world and is recovering sensory input from your subconscious. What you accomplish is not only a way to self-mastery, but you are open to all sorts of other things like psychic impressions. Those who meditate regularly, experience higher energy levels, lower blood pressure and reduced stress. During meditation, your brain activity levels (BAL) decrease from beta (everyday; wide awake) to alpha (asleep; drowsy or relaxed). Learning this is healthy all around. A focused mind can accomplish tasks more efficiently and process challenges more clearly. This state allows your mind to work with the Divine Source connection within you in the present moment always, allowing for highly lucid interactions with life. True inner peace ensues.

"Through intense deep meditation you reach a state that is beyond thought, beyond change, beyond imagination, beyond differences and duality. Once you can stay in that state for a while and come out of it without losing any of it, then the inner divine love will

begin to pour through you. You will not see people as different, separate individuals. You will see your own Self in everyone around you. Then the flow of love from within you will be constant and unbroken."
~ Swami Muktananda

Chapter 14

Breath Awareness

Create space with breath. As you focus only on your breath your attention to mind thoughts goes away and you are in the present moment allowing space and stillness to be there. Breathing, in and of itself, holds the key to our divine connection. For without breathing we would not survive. Become aware of your breath in every moment. Your breath is always in the present. Breath awareness is most powerful and transformational.

Breath is the key to relaxation. Pranayama is a Sanskrit word that means lengthening of the prana or breath. Prana is life force or vital energy. Pranayama yoga is a practice of control of breath. Prana itself is the essence and energy of God/ Divine itself. It is everywhere. It is in the trees, the flowers, the sun and it is vital to our very survival. That is why we are so linked with Mother Nature.

Breathe . . . I've seen profound results in just breathing through your intention and feeling it. Breathe very deeply in and very slowly out. Use the full capacity of your lungs. Be with the sound and rhythm of your breath. Become aware of your breath and most especially at the tail end of your out-breath. There is a stillness and energy here. Focus on your breath for a time. Feel the energy body within you expand. Breathe and then your focus is on the intention while allowing the energy to flow to you and through you. You are focusing only on the present moment. In this present moment your power resides. When in this present state of mind you can pinpoint and focus on your desired goal. Be focused and enjoy the divine energy flowing to you always. Remember what you focus upon expands. So focus on the positive elements of love, peace and joy as you intend! Enjoy the breathing in the present moment!

As stated in *Heart of Yoga* by T.K.V. Desikachar, "An emphasis on long inhalation and holding the breath after inhalation intensified the effects of a yoga posture in the chest area and supports the elimination process and has a cleansing affect on the body by enlivening the organs, especially abdominal region. An emphasis on long exhalation and holding the breath after exhalation intensifies the effects of the posture in the abdominal region (energized and heats the body)."

There are a variety of powerful ways that you can practice pranayama yoga to benefit your entire body. The use of pranayama techniques are very beneficial for smoothing out Kundalini symptoms that are too intense. Some forms I am come across are: Quiet breathing, Deep breathing, fast breathing, spinal breathing and many others with names I simply cannot pronounce. When practicing these versions of breathing it is imperative to your health that you do these with proper guidance and follow the instructions given. For the sake of this book, I will only be getting into the more natural techniques of deep breathing, fast breathing (ex. Breath of Fire), Quiet breathing and simply breath awareness for blissful present moment living.

"Breathe. Let go. And remind yourself that this very moment is the only one you know you have for sure."
~ Oprah Winfrey

Breath awareness is a beautiful meditation to practice wherever you are. Just breathe and be aware of the breath. Watch your breath. Come into the present moment. As you breathe in, be with the inhale. As you breathe out, be with the exhale. You will find your inner calm a comforting place to be that is strangely familiar. Energy is our life force. It has been called Prana, Chi, Ki, etc. When we breathe we take in oxygen and life force energy to survive. As you breathe in, you are taking in Light and Energy. Let's call it **Light Breathing!** Simply be aware that your breath is powerful and causes subtle but noticeable shifts from within.

Breathe FULLY! Breathe DEEPLY. Breathe **deep belly breaths.** Breathe deeply using the full capacity of your lungs and then take time to really feel your stomach filling with air. Feel the rhythm of your breath. Fall into this rhythm and allow it to soothe you. When we were babies we knew how to breathe correctly and fully. Watch a baby breathing. Their belly goes out and in. Stop focusing on how you look and breathe. Feel most comfortable from within. Most of us move into breathing through our chests and lungs still never taking a full breath. So when you become conscious of the power of breath awareness, take those moments to breathe deeply and fully. Even watch your lungs and belly inflate and then deflate. Deep, slow, full breaths are key to really bringing in the energy to your body in beautiful most healthy ways. You will truly feel the difference immediately. This is a process to condition yourself back to breathing healthily and also uplifts the energy. Some yogi's out there have a goal to have less numbers of breaths per minute. So instead of 20 breaths per minute you can reduce it to four long deep full healing breaths per minute. And you can work your way towards this goal over a long period of time. But don't worry about the number just breathe fully and deeply. Disease is carried away with the breath. So allow your body to come back to its natural innate breathing rhythm. Do this full breath process and also simply practice breath awareness of natural rhythm breathing without force. Both bring profound results.

I've been lucky enough to have attended a workshop to learn a **Full-Wave® Breathing** technique with Linda Jaros at the Life Breath Wellness Center in East Greenwich, Rhode Island. The Full-Wave® Breathing technique was created by Dr. Tom Goode. This is much like I just explained with breathing naturally like a baby but with a new awareness. Breathe in deep through your nose into your lower belly, then your middle belly or diaphragm and then fill your lungs. Then immediately exhale it all out naturally through the mouth. It doesn't have to be a long slow exhale, just release it out. Let it all go. And without holding your breath at the top or bottom of breaths, keep the flow going. Inhale low in belly to chest, filling your lungs and exhale even with a sigh if you like. Try this technique daily for at least 10 breathe or even for 20-45 minutes (if you have the time) for 30 days. You will be amazed at the results in your body, mind and spirit. Upon the first time trying this technique, my body began to tremble with shakes or tremors. These weren't like tingles from extra oxygen (that I was receiving also). These were real Kundalini activated trembles and shakes. It was fun to witness. As you do this technique you are, also, working with and rising up the Kundalini energy within you.

There is also a yoga **Breath of Fire** technique to achieve higher states while shedding energy blockages. It's a fast paced breath that is known for assisting in releasing a lot of negative energies. In this technique you take in fast balanced inhales through your nose and fast balanced exhales out of your nose. This technique of fast sharp breaths removes heavy, stagnant energy from our bodies. A way to assist you in practicing this is to first have your mouth open and stick your tongue kind of like a dog and breathe very fast in and out. Then when you are ready, close your mouth and do this fast breathing through your nostrils. There is no pushing or pulling. You'll simply feel a pull in your solar plexus area and possibly a root lock feeling at the root chakra level. Remember this is fast breathing in and out of your nose in equal time. Keep the breath equal. Don't actually

try for the Breath of Fire. There is no trying. With Breath of
Fire you are natural, easy, fluid and powerful. No pushing or
pulling of stomach or diaphragm or chest. Just quick, fast, easy
breathing. Find a good rhythm and fall into it.

You can also do this technique standing. Stand, arms easily
at sides. Shake your body, really let it all out. Then jump body
up and down fast and short in rhythm with your breathing
through the nose. This aids in movement and breath while
visualizing Kundalini rising if you like. You can also do the
Breath of Fire while sitting comfortably and with legs crossed.
Hold your arms up, thumbs out, and all other fingers facing
in at the first joint. Close your eyes and do the Breathe of Fire
for as long as you can, then hold it for longer. Breathing with
movement is very powerful. And in movements, such as Yoga,
breath is a key factor in keeping rhythm and to, also, achieve
what goals you are setting up for the yogic practice. Yoga is
has great balancing benefits for incorporating the combination
of breath and movement.

To bring the Breath of Fire to an advanced level the
technique is the same, you just increase the power and the pace
within which you breathe. So you can move to intermediate or
advanced for extra pace and power. During this breath you are
naturally pulsating your lower regions, naturally waking and
stirring your Kundalini. Energy pathways start to open up and
you start to get vitalized. You will notice changes immediately
as you practice this pranayama. Practice. The Breath of Fire
magnifies benefits of any exercise when used in conjunction
with the exercise! Do not practice the Breath of Fire if you are
Kundalini awakened or going through terrible symptoms, as
it can aggravate or enhance the process. In such cases, only
practice this under the specific guidance of a guru or wise
teacher.

I've given you three options: Full Belly Breathing, Natural
Rhythm Breathing (or breath awareness) and fast Breath of Fire
breathing techniques. There are other breath techniques that
assist you in holding your breath in for a few moments. While
you hold your breath you are sustaining the life force within
just a little bit longer. This is very healing. One such technique

that uses the option of holding the breath is called Alternate Nostril Breathing. **Alternate nostril breathing technique** is a yogic technique that I highly recommend to assist you through Kundalini symptoms. Alternate nostril breathing is said to relieve heat and cold symptoms. This is also beneficial as a preface to symptoms and will assist in balancing out what would have been a harsh symptom.

It is much easier to do this while watching another guiding you. Your hand is held in front of your nose, you will alternate your thumb and pinky finger to block one nostril at a time. Each inhale and exhale is done slowly to the count of four. If desiring a cooling affect, block your right nostril first and breathe in through your left nostril (to the count of 1, 2, 3, 4). Then block your left nostril and breathe out through your right nostril (1, 2, 3, 4). Then block the left nostril and breathe out through the right nostril (1, 2, 3, 4). Leaving your left nostril blocked, breathe in through the right nostril (1, 2, 3, 4). Block the right nostril and breathe out through the left nostril (1, 2, 3, 4). Repeat the cycle of alternate-nostril breathing a few times and end the cycle with an exhale through the left nostril. For a warming effect, begin your first inhale through the right nostril and finish the cycle by exhaling through your right nostril.

There are many other various breathing techniques through yoga that you can explore. Enjoy the process!

As you take a few minutes a day to consciously breathe you build a beautiful reserve of life force energy within. I'm finding it's most beneficial to focus on the spaces between breaths. The space between is most sacred. A blissful stillness is here. For me it seems highly beneficial to focus on the breathing out (exhale) for bringing in beautiful energy to self and others. There is a space between that occurs on the in-breath (inhale) as well as the out-breath (exhale). This space seems quite pivotal in building the energy. I will do a lot of visualization and energies on the holding of breath after an exhale before breathing back in. Another method is to pause on the in-breath as well as the out-breath. This brings your mind inward. Your thoughts wither away and you feel the divine connection. Practice this method as often as you like. Do what feels good for you during this process and every day!

Gerd Lange has puts the importance of prana and breathing into perspective when he says, "In general, there are two things which we take in when we breathe. One is air and the other is prana, pure life-force energy itself, more vital than air for our existence. If you take away air, you have a couple of minutes before you die; if you take away water, you have even more time; and if you take away food you have much more time still, but if you break prana from spirit, death is instantaneous. So taking in prana with breath is absolutely crucial in sustaining our life."

Taking full deep breaths, in and out, assist us in taking in the Divine life force energy completely. The feeling is tremendous. Rebirthing is also a beautiful form of breathwork for profound transformations. I strongly suggest sampling rebirthing techniques from a certified Rebirther near you.

Working with breathwork is so powerful. And also when you incorporate the energy consciously within the breath you feel the rejuvenating affects. Expert Rebirther, Sondra Ray, explains the vital-ness of energy and breath: "Breathwork, or conscious breathing, is a physical, mental and spiritual experience. The physical part consists of connecting your inhale and exhale in a relaxed rhythm (with no holding at the top or bottom). The spiritual dimension of conscious breathing is the heart of the matter. One purpose of breathwork is not only the movement of air but also the movement of ENERGY."

So I invite you to breathe deeply, consciously and be here now.

Chapter 15

Stand in the Earth

Grounding

We are of the stars and we are also of the Earth. We must remain balanced both in the stars and in Mother Earth. We are connected with both. We are living on this planet in this dimension for many reasons and lessons. So it is helpful to live here and stay connected out there in harmony. Too much of being in the heavens gets you further away from living your life here in the temple God gave you that we call a body. The benefits are coming from both worlds. We can be in balance and harmony with both worlds.

Keeping your center is easiest when grounded. Signs you're not grounded: Klutzy, forgetful, "Not with it", "In the clouds"—Keeping in mind that these signs go over and beyond what you are normally. And a major sign of not being grounded is if you are not in the present moment, but are too caught up in the past or worrying about the future. Whenever you are feeling fear on any level you are not grounded. If you are thinking about something that happened in the past and regretting it, you are not grounded and are in fear. If you are thinking too much about what might happen in the future and are worrying, you are not grounded and are in fear. Breathe and do the steps below.

Grounding is imperative to release energy from within and throughout your bodies system. As Kundalini rises we have much more energy that seems electrical. We affect lights, computers and other electrical appliances. If you are noticing anything electrical around you going haywire, you could be in some high electrical Kundalini energies. First ground yourself! Then protect your belongings by putting a protective bubble around them with intention of proper functioning and protection from the Divine.

Grounding assists you in staying in the present moment and in connection with the Divine. A constant state of surrender and allowing is amazingly easy when grounded.

Many Ways to ground:

- Grounding visualizations (such as picturing yourself as a tree) are my favorite and one of the most effective ways to bring me to a grounded state. You can do this anytime and anywhere. Below is one example of a quick Grounding visualization for you to utilize: Visualize your feet planted firmly on the ground (whether they are or not, even laying down for meditation). Then picture each of them attached to white/silver cords. These cords send Light from your entire being through your feet to the ground. From here your white/silver cord spirals downward as far as you can imagine, to the CORE of Earth. You can send all negative thoughts, emotions, worries and experiences on down this cord to the Core. Here you see your cord (as well as many others from around the globe) secured to a beautiful round crystal, shining full of White Shining Light like millions of diamonds combined. As your cord secures in this crystal, these negative energies are transmuted into white pure energy. You then see a beautiful BURST of light that sends the Light back up the cords, watching it spiral upwards toward you again. It finally reaches you (in as much time that is comfortable for you) and the light goes through your feet, up your calves, thighs, stomach area, chest, arms, neck and head, through your Crown Chakra—seeing the light go out to the Universe. See and feel the light within you expand outward. You are now grounded and connected. Now, this can take as long or as short of time as you would like it to. The more you practice this; you will find it only takes seconds to ground yourself.

- Grounding out high energy by sending or running the energy to the Earth. Send your negative emotions to the Earth for transmutation. Angel, hate, fear, anxiety, etc. The Daily Om has another option of how to do this, "To begin, sit and breathe deeply, ask Mother Earth to accept your anger, and imagine it coming down your spine out of your tailbone, and into the earth's deep core. To finish, be sure to honor and thank the earth for her loving service." Then when you've released all the ick feel the spaciousness within you. And then, send love to the earth every day. It feels good!!! Run the energy to a school, church, town. Release it. If you've done this as long as you think you can and you are still filled with a lot of energy and the other grounding techniques aren't working, sometimes it's simply best to surrender to it and ride the wave.
- Stop Meditating
- Decrease all forms of concentration (shorter reading times, shorter prayer time, etc.)
- Steer clear of alcohol, caffeine and drugs

- Walking, walking and more walking.
- Stomp the bottoms of your heels on the ground.
- Rub salt on arms from top (shoulder) to bottom (hands). Then rinse with cold water.
- Use salt in a cold shower or bath.
- Even washing your hands for 60 seconds is a great grounding too. While washing your hands you can also visualize all the outside energies that are not yours leaving and going down the drain.
- Walking has tremendous benefits to our mind, body and soul. It is also very grounding. When you are walking you are connecting directly to Mother Earth.
- Hug a tree.
- Simply being outside in nature and breathing in the natural life of planet earth is tremendously grounding, cleansing and connecting on many spiritual layers.
- Eat food. Meat tends to be heavy if you really need extra grounding. (Don't forget to bless your food to rid it of any painful energies that might be in there. You do not want to ingest that karma.)
- Be around Children. Their playfulness gets you right down with them and having a great time!
- Do light-hearted mundane everyday tasks.
- Get your hands into gardening. You're in the Earth! What better way to truly ground than to get into the nitty gritty of the dirt and plants of the Earth through gardening.
- Press two fingers hard on your back by your Heart Chakra on either side of your spine. (This will have to be done by a friend.)
- Forms of creative release can be wonderfully grounding. Writing, drawing, sculpting are great for releasing issues that will arise and a great side-effect is getting grounded. Sometimes as you awaken you'll notice a lot of energy and this is an excellent way to release it.

Chapter 16

Get up and Move

Movement, breath and sound are powerful ways that work together in clearing energy blockages and stagnant mental and emotional energy from the mind, body and soul.

Our bodies were made to move! Movement allows our bodies to flow and revitalizes our entire system! The blood and oxygen flows more smoothly. Our joints need to open up and loosen in order for energy to flow through easily. This assists us in our awakenings tremendously. Movement allows our bodies to release that which would have remained stagnant. The energy flows! Be aware of your body and the messages you receive from it. As you move and release what comes up in the moment, it no longer manifests in the body as sickness or dis-ease. As you stretch and move, you release old stored up, pushed down emotions and stagnant energy that is locked away in our body; prior experiences that we may not have fully released or processed. Emotions such as sadness, anxiety, anger, frustration and fear are all locked into the body when we don't allow these to be naturally processed in the present moment. When we move we may notice emotions coming up for final release. It's truly an energetic release as well as a physical one. Pure magic occurs and we realize moving is what is innate within us.

When I originally decided to finally dedicate my life to exercises daily, I hadn't realized that I was also contributing to my spiritual goals. I realize the power of this divine decision now. The Divine took over for me. Gone were those lazy days of overeating and complacency. I worked on shedding pounds and raising my vibrations unaware that the two were integrated. Movement releases tension and karma that is held within you.

There's more. Moving while visualizing is truly very powerful indeed. Be aware of the body as you flow through this sacred process. Move it if you feel the desire to do so. I've found it helpful to be sure my body is stretched out with all the kinks worked through. Move each joint (Neck, shoulders, hips, spine, knees and ankles) in circular motions one at a time. Be aware of the flow of energy. But most importantly just move your body. I feel our divine connection is through our Body, Mind and Soul. And to truly feel that connection we need to move our body, breathe and connect to the Divine through energy and meditation. Knowing that as we allow our body to move and come into a stillness for meditation it's accomplished with more ease than if we had simply just tried to meditate without allowing the energy to be released from the body through movement.

Dancing is a powerful connection to the Source within you. As you dance you are moving your body and feeling a rhythm deep within your soul. You need not worry about perfect choreography for soul dancing. Just move your body however you enjoy. Playing trance dance music or any music that feels uplifting to your soul is strongly recommended. As you do this you are free. When you move your body, you forget the world and you remember yourself. You remember you are graceful, beautiful, and strong. And you always have been! You remember your true divine nature. You remember your connection and therefore feel it in a higher way. You raise your vibrations as you dance! Free your mind. Free your body. Free your soul.

The movement of your choice may be walking, aerobics, yoga, dance, Tai Chi, Qi Gong exercise, bicycling, drumming, strength training, stretch, etc. and a combination of everything! My Husband's drum sessions are a full cardio routine for him! Try to choose something that moves your entire body if you can. Whatever your choice as long as you are moving your body, it is receiving benefits that go beyond physical improvements. Amazing connections are made easier with movement.

There is a myth by many that you need to practice yoga in order to have a Kundalini awakening. You don't need to practice yoga for Divine (Shakti) connections to happen. But, yes, Yoga will assist with this goal along with other practices. Yoga has been found in eastern religions to truly smooth out the Kundalini process. Yoga brings a mind-body connection. Not only this, but the tension release in the muscles assists in clearing karma. I highly recommend experiencing yoga asanas and all forms of yoga in its highest spiritual form. I've heard many stories of those with a raging Kundalini using Yoga to smooth out the process. These people find yoga beneficial for the physical aspects of Kundalini awakenings as well as the emotional and mental upheavals. As you move and breathe you are brought to a higher place within yourself where you are the Divine and nothing else can touch this place.

I love doing yoga. It feels so good for my mind, body and soul! Yoga means "union" and is a way of releasing the mind to just Be. The goal of yoga is self awareness. Yoga involves breathing, physical body movements and states of awareness that naturally evolve as you progress. I recommend any healthy form of body movement daily. I find this to be an imperative part to connecting with the Divine. As I move and breathe my body remains healthy and my joints and meridians are cleared of blockages. We are all ascending and we are all raising our vibrations to the higher frequencies in conjunction with the Divine Mother Earth. You will be drawn to do different things that keep you in line with your path. Yoga is a beautiful option for moving your body and activating your light body! So, too, are Tai Chi and Qi Gong. The energy is incorporated in with breath and movement. The energy powerfully builds and emanates with these options. These are amazing and beautiful moving meditations. Just allow, be and see what flows your way. We are all unique, so we will all have unique methods that will work for us.

I've made some observations of the aerobic workout I practice. The workouts of my choice are Denise Austin's aerobic workouts and Chalene's *Turbo Fire*. Denise and Chalene's workouts are my joy in exercising. Their unique workouts are upbeat with beautiful energy and pure joy. They are infused with multi-dimensional movements for us multi-dimensional beings. They both integrate the right and left brain together with movements that go to the left and the right, up and down. Your body is constantly changing and moving. The workouts are filled with sports moves, dance moves, kickboxing, Tai Chi, Pilates, Yoga and stretching. The breath goes from fast in and out to slow and easy. These bear striking resemblance the yogic Breath of Fire and Long Deep Breathing techniques. Movement and breath are extremely important for our soul and honoring our divine physical bodies. Moving and stretching allows our joints to loosen up so energy can flow through much easier. I now enjoy working out daily after my rituals of energy and meditation. These I do right when I wake up in the morning before the rest of my day begins. I am centered and focused.

Walking is one of the easiest, and most often discussed, as the highest benefit throughout your Kundalini awakening. Not only is walking an excellent grounding technique, it also assists with your physical body in moving parts that are not usually used. Walking requires breathing and you can even do rhythmic breathing while walking for different benefits depending on your goals. (Check out the chapter called *Breath Awareness*. I share the yogic Breath of Fire exercise that you may want to try while walking.) I remember a few years ago where for at least a 4 months stretch I was doing my usual morning workout, an extra workout at night and walking at least three miles a day, five or more days a week. I realize now how intense that was. I have read other ascension people having walking many more miles every day. There are inner levels of releasing and processing going on just as you simply walk. Walking truly does benefit the mind, body and soul.

Dance! Dancing any way that feels good to our body allows our right brain to integrate into our logical left brain more and release pent up energies, feeling free! Release! Release! Release! Rhythm is inherent in each of us. You know this just by watching a toddler start to move to the beat of a song playing. We are meant to move our bodies free. I have my own Joy dance I like to do every day. Just by taking a few minutes every day I lift my spirits. Sometimes I have to do my joy dance more than once, but it's worth it to let out all the energy that builds up; especially if the energy that built up brought you to a negative or lower vibration mood. Get up and dance! Lift your arms up, move your legs and be free. You can do this in the bathroom at work too! Don't forget to smile at yourself in the mirror before you leave the bathroom. And remember it's impossible to stay in a bad mood when your arms are lifted high in the air and your face is up and smiling! They have done studies to prove this. So give it a shot! It's happiness you are bringing to you even more. Yay!

There is another way to move that is so simple, it sounds silly. It's **shaking**. Kim Engh brought this to me and I LOVE IT! This is a beautiful Qi Gong method that Kim Engh shared during a seminar I attended that removes residue and that ick energy from your body. She said during her awakening process she was doing this daily or several times a day. And I'm finding that I'm doing this every day this week and it's really helping me a lot. It's removed a lot of blockages and energy needing to be releasing.

Start with Shaking your hand fast and furious. Then your hand and arm and then hand, upper arm and should. Then do the same on the other side. And move to your feet. Start with your left foot shaking vigorously. Then shake your foot, and knee. And then the whole leg. Move to the other side. Then bring your arms and legs and whole body into shaking up and down, slow at first and picking up the pace into almost jumping. Start shaking your head a bit too. Then get really into it and jump up and down, arms up high and shaking. Really let go. The Letting go is the most important part of this too. Let loose! Let it all go! Then stick your tongue way out and say, "Blaaaaah" to the air around you. Do this three times or however many times you want. Shake it, shake it, shake it! When you feel like you've really released and let go of a lot, stop. Observe your body. Stand straight and strong, arms and legs straight and activated in Mountain pose (feet hip width apart flat on the floor, back elongated, head is pulling up as if an energy is assisting it in reaching the sky). Feel the beautiful numbness and tingling sensations in your body. Feel the hum in your body when you've completed a shaking session. Feel the aliveness that you are. Close your eyes and breathe into this beautiful sensation.

Movement and body language speak. Our physical body position sends messages to our brains. When you hold your body in an upright and powerful position you feel good and send that message to your brain. Likewise, if you are in a weak body position you send that message to your brain.

Try this body exercise. Stand up, feet equally placed on the floor together, hold your hands up high and smile. How do you feel? Now put your hands down, frown, corners at your mouth turned down, slouch your shoulders and rest on one hip. Now how do you feel? Okay, now hands back up, breathing in and smiling. Try to feel down or angry. It's downright impossible isn't it? Put your hands back down, frown, slouch and balance on one hip. Try to feel happy or ecstatic. Pretty hard to do right? Finish this exercise with your hands back up, smiling and breathing. Jump for joy! Stand strong, feeling good, strong, a child of the universe. Our physical body position sends messages to our subconscious. Shifting our body can shift our consciousness. Carry yourself as if you were a sacred vessel, an incredible life force energy flowing through every cell of your body. Because you are!

Find your "Joy" body position. Find your happy body position. Find your love body position. Learn it, use it, modify it and reuse it daily! Use your body to bring you into alignment with the feeling you are to manifest. If you are slouching with your head down it is hard to be in an uplifting joy-filled mood, that you so desire to manifest. Bring your body into alignment by raising your head up high, lifting your arms to the Universe and honoring yourself! By doing this (and there have been studies) you are bringing your body into alignment with higher vibrating emotions and it's impossible to feel down. If you do this daily, you bring yourself and your subconscious into DAILY habits of feeling this emotion to the point where you will consistently attract the positive emotions you are wanting to manifest. "Acting as if" is assisting greatly just by using your body! I jump up and down daily and feel utter complete JOY. Since starting this I have felt happier and more joyful and attract more joy-filled experiences and I know this is one of the many things I have done that assisted this in happening. I brought my vibrations in alignment with bringing this to me now!

No matter where you are, YOU can feel good! You deserve to feel good, no matter what others are feeling, no matter what the conditioning or beliefs are. You are meant to feel good. Do not resist good feelings! No more! What you resist persists. You will attract negative experiences if you stay in negative body positions that enhance negative moods, so change your body position. Be in your loving power! Embrace positive happy emotions. If you feel like smiling, smile! Keep telling yourself daily that your life is blessed now!

It's been proven scientifically that our body's chemistry gets addicted to emotion. So even if we don't like feeling down, we will keep doing things to attract that emotion because we are addicted. (What the bleep helps explain this.) There are no victims only volunteers. Create receptor sites to get addicted to feeling good! We get used to our comfort zones, so start moving and release those comfort zones and fire up new receptors in our brain to train our subconscious to create experiences to keep that emotion going. Make joy a comfort zone! Again use your body to shift your emotional state.

They've done tests on split personalities. One personality could have an allergic reaction to bees and one would not. One might have diabetes and one would not. As the personality changes the blood work changes in the person. There is power in identity. Some would rather die than not be in alignment with identity. So start to shift your consciousness through meditation, visuals, movement, breath, sound, touch, etc. Bring your consciousness to higher vibrations and move into a new reality of miracles.

Chapter 17

Connect With Nature

Get out in nature. Drink in the air, the sun, the beauty, the aliveness and the presence of living peacefully in the Now no matter what is happening while connecting with nature. Become truly present with nature as you enjoy it. Stand strong, breathe, ground and connect. Connect with the Earth as much as you can. As you commune with nature you align with the natural rhythms of Earth. And you remember the divine being that you are. Your connection is enhanced as you are with nature. We are all one. I enjoy daily walks in nature. To breathe in the life of the sky, wind, trees and water is truly unique and awakening. You become one with all that is when in nature. You realize that nothing that is happening is bigger than the peace of nature. Nature is crucial to our survival. We can honor its presence and it honors ours. As you are out in nature, everything else falls away.

They have done studies on hospital patients; where one patient will be in a room with only the four plain walls and one patient has a window with a view of nature. The patient who had the view of nature recovered faster. This same study was performed on a patient who had four walls and only a picture of nature. This patient recovered almost as fast or just as fast as the patient who had the window view of nature. These are amazing results!

The sun is truly energizing. The sun clears, energizes and rejuvenates your body from the inside out. Take in a few sun breaths and allow the sun energy to wash over you and through you. Immense benefits are felt on all levels, physically, mentally, emotionally and spiritually when you are exposed to the sun. The sun is Shiva or masculine energy. We need this as much as we need Shakti or feminine energy. There have been studies done about people who live in areas of tremendous rain and low sun exposure. There is a higher percentage of depression and anxiety in these places in the world. And on the flip side, those who are exposed to the sun pretty much daily are happier and more energized. So if you are lucky to have the sun in your daily life, bask in it. Enjoy it as much as you can. I discuss in Book 2: *Divine Embrace* a method called Sungazing that you may be intrigued with.

We must have our yin with our yang. The moon is our feminine aspect and like the sun fills us with so much energy. The moon is our feminine cycle. I feel more energized during full moon periods (waxing) then when the moon is waning. We each resonate within our cycle uniquely. Take some time to see where you receive rejuvenation while enjoying exploring natures wonders.

A shift occurs the moment you step out and connect with nature. It is majestic and true. Suddenly you can breathe more fully. Issues fall away and you remember we are as the trees are; true Divine energy itself.

I walk outside in nature as often as I can. I try to do it daily. There are beautiful paths where I work and I just got lost in the trees, birds and air. I get lost remembering this is truly what it's all about. I get grounded. I am just me. Life is simple. I am. Life truly is simple. It is easier to just BE, when in nature.

Nature never worries about the small things. Nature just stays in the flow of what is happening right now and knows that it is always taken care of. The awareness comes back to us that there is nothing wrong. There never was. There is nothing to do and no where to go. Just being here and now is all there is. We are truly blessed. And the more we take time to notice these precious blessing-filled moments the more we will experience them.

Chapter 18

Body Awareness

Body Awareness & Detoxification

L isten to your body. Talk to your body. Honor your physical and energy bodies. Our bodies never lie and always send us messages of how it is feeling. We are in tune with what our body needs and all we need to do is realize this and talk with it. Most illness is due to our disconnection with our spiritual/ energy and physical bodies.

We have been conditioned to listen only to logic and mind conditioning instead of hearing what our spiritual self and energy bodies are trying to say to us. If we ignore a subtle message it will be come stronger. Remember, listen to the whispers or hear the screams of your body. Check in with your body every day. Ask your body what it needs and you will get answers. Illness and nature comes into our lives as a way to let us know when we are not listening to our guidance system. So thank the illness, bacteria and even insects for showing you the misalignment that you've manifested. Let them know you've got the message now and tune in to your body.

If you feel you are not able to listen quite yet, call on your Angels for assistance and clarity. They will send you signs and messages to assist you and empower you to heal. When you honor its messages you feel energized and at ease. Staying conscious of what's happening within our body will allow us to take active steps in remaining healthy rather than waiting till it's too late and has manifested in the body.

I am starting to listen to my physical body this week and have included more corn, spinach and carrots to my diet and (oh no!) less chocolate! ☺ I feel so much better and at least right now am not craving more than what I have because I've replaced those chocolate binges with eating veggies and I still allow myself a snack at night too (of a Healthy Choice chocolate ice-cream bar). What you bring in to your physical body flows into your energy bodies and vice versa. Pay attention to the subtle energy shifts within your body. You will feel certain twinges, aches and pains; some physical and some energetic. Ask your body for the message and honor the truth and wisdom the body gives you. Your body never lies, so listen up. Body awareness is not only very healing to the self on all levels but is also a great grounding method. By being in touch with how you are feeling right now it truly brings you back to the present moment and all of the gifts it holds.

Body detoxification is eradicating your physical body of all those elements that are no longer serving your highest and best, good. As you rid your physical body of unnecessary toxins you also raise your vibrations and assist your ascension symptoms in feeling more balanced and harmonious. As you are clear your surroundings will feel clear and you will more easily face issues in your life in more balanced peaceful ways. Each person's diet will be different. Each person has a body that is unique to them. But something that remains consistent is to drink as much water as you can; at least and even more than eight glasses of water a day. You really are releasing much in this ascension process and water greatly assists your body, heals your body, and releases many toxins just by drinking water. I try to drink at least eight glasses of water a day and some days even more. If you are feeling thirsty, then you are already dehydrated, so get a glass of water. You can do something fun with the water and visualize beautiful energy being infused in the water and that same beautiful sparkling water (of any color you choose) is then infusing YOU with new rejuvenating life force energy. You *will* feel the results.

Another tip (that I received from Chrism of www. KundaliniAwakeningSystems1.com) is to eat watermelon every day. This is filled with water and is also a beautiful cleanser of the kidneys. The kidneys are commonly hit hard during some Kundalini ascension symptoms stages and eating the watermelon will greatly alleviate the strain on the kidneys and keep them running strong. What a great tip! I love watermelon so this suggestion will be easy to follow.

We cannot say that one person must go into an all raw fruit and vegetable diet if their particular body requires certain proteins found in meat. We cannot say that all persons require a fasting. Each person will follow this divine path to detoxify their body the way they are drawn to. Remember, you can also ask your Higher Self and your Angels to assist you in clearing your body of toxins. They are working with you and by doing this, if you so choose, this allows them to more easily channel through you. A stronger connection ensues. Your Angels and Higher Self know specifically what you need to do and what you can handle. You will receive many signs and synchronicities along the way that will tell you and help you figure out what you need to do. A lot of you will gradually get to a good place within yourself and your body. Just follow the signs and you will get there. Find your way.

Generally, a rule of thumb is to rid yourself of all intake of: caffeine, chocolate, wine, sugars, processed food (pretty much everything in a box), alcohol and drugs. Over time I've found that I have limited my intake of caffeine and just recently stopped entirely. This was over the span of 4-5 years. I did not go cold turkey. I prefer to do things when I feel ready and it just happened. I saw signs from the Angels and the Divine that led me to stop coffee intake as much as possible. (I occasionally still have a cup, but rarely.) As your Kundalini symptoms persist you may notice that it is helpful to have high protein intake every two to three hours during waking hours. Some weeks I am eating more than I usually do and others I am back to what I consider "normal". And some weeks I am big on buying all kinds of nuts for their wonderful nutrients and protein. I am doing my best to go with the flow and follow the messages from my body and the signs that are presented to me. Again it is what feels best for you. We are each experiencing ascension in our own unique ways.

I have had at least one diet Dr. Pepper a day for, at least, three years. And only recently have I stopped for good now. It's actually been about a year now! I remembered just this weekend when I unconsciously ordered the usual Diet Coke from Wendy's Restaurant only to sit down at the table and clearly see a sprite in front of me. I took the hint. I must admit I am still a regular chocolate eater but it is slowly dwindling to a more balanced intake! I do believe that if you do things in moderation, you should be okay. Just listen to your body. If you know that when you eat certain foods, you don't feel so well afterwards, stop eating them. If you haven't figured those things out yet, ask your body. Talk to your body and it will answer you. A knowing, a feel, or a thought just comes to you. Remember, to ask your Higher Self, your body and your Angels for guidance and assistance in shedding yourself of the foods that no longer serve you. You will find yourself feeling more energized and lighter.

Remember our thoughts and emotions can uplift our bodies' energies or cause detriment and illness. So be aware of your thoughts and always remain in the highest vibration possible. A great book that goes into great depth about this and physical immortality is *How to be Chic, Fab and Live Forever* by Sondra Ray. You can change your body to be and stay in a healthy state of being. You can remain younger than mass consciousness leads you to believe. We've fallen into the trap that our bodies must die in order for ascension to occur. Now we can work on ridding ourselves of the conditioned thoughts and stay out of negative mass consciousness thinking. You can train your thoughts. You can shine your light bright within and beam health and vitality.

A major part of our body that we must bring our awareness to is our skin. Our skin is one of the largest detoxing organs of our body. So it's very important to keep our skin clean and breathing freely to work properly. One of the best ways to do this is practicing dry brushing. This is exactly what it sounds like. Taking a hard bristled brush made for dry brushing and brushing the skin, every inch of our body. This assists the lymph system and removes dead skin as well as toxins that have naturally risen to the surface of the skin for release. It has also been known to reduce cellulite build-up. This is a wonderful positive. Another positive is dry skin brushing reduced dry sky! How wonderful is that. For someone with bouts of eczema I am happy to have a new method to leave the itchy dry skin issues behind!

I first heard of dry skin brushing from Denise Linn in 2008 when I attended her Soul Coaching Training at her home in San Luis Obispo, California. From there this has been popping up into my awareness from time to time. So I'm going to listen to the signs that have been coming and finally begin a regular dry skin brushing practice.

How to perform dry skin brushing: It's recommended we do this every day. But do it as often as you can. Don't beat yourself up and give up. Keep up the good practice for yourself. We take the dry brush (that is found inexpensive at local health stores) and begin brushing the skin. There are several methods of brushing found online. You can research this to see what resonates with you. But mostly you just brush every inch of your body till you've covered it all. Then it's helpful to jump right into the shower and wash away all that has been removed from the dry brushing.

Let's run through all the positive reasons for doing something that only take a few minutes a day. *Dry skin brushing:*

1. is great for the immunity by allowing the lymph to flow properly.
2. assists the body to absorb vitamins, more specifically vitamins A, D, E an d K, where our body needs them most.
3. assists the lymphatic system to detox from the inside out. And as I mentioned removing dead skin cells from the body rejuvenates the skin and allows it to move more toxins out of the body.
4. is exfoliating, removing all the dead skin off the surface so the naturally moisturized skin is on the surface.
5. breaks through cellulite buildup and tightens up the skin with regular dry skin brushing over time (3-6 months to see a difference.) This also triggers nerve endings at the surface of the skin which tones the associated muscles.
6. is invigorating to the skin and refreshing the body for a more aliveness feel
7. prevents Cancer. As the author (name unknown) of the blog dryskinbrush.blogspot.com states, "We have cancerous cells in our bodies all the time. A tumor grows when our body is unable to detect and kill these cells that have started to become poisonous to our bodies. A big function of the lymphatic system is to show foreign materials to the immune system. This includes parts of cancer cells. If the lymph is flowing the immune system can detect cancers early and clear them."
8. stimulated the hormone producing glands which largely maintain metabolism and levels of chemicals in the blood.

Chapter 19

Appreciation, Gratitude and Love

Come to a place of Appreciation, Gratitude and Love. Appreciation, gratitude and Love are high vibrational frequencies that allow you to be in a higher way of being, untouchable.

Things will still go on around you but you will not feel the stresses or fear of them. There is no need to be in the ego state of mind. Simply allow and feel appreciation and gratitude. The shift within your frequency will be powerful and instantaneous. You will face challenges in your life from a better, more centered, grounded state of mind. From this state you can also create manifestations in a higher way.

Start with the little things around you. Keep your focus on those beautiful wonders, such as a baby sleeping in your arms, laughter, a bubble bath, the smell of nature, the sounds of nature, etc. These little things are here for us to enjoy. Take that appreciation and build upon it, let it grow within you! As you come to your Inner Peace you are accessing the higher dimensions within yourself. Awakening to what has always been there.

"Appreciation is a key that will unlock the doorway to the new world, even as the old world dissolves and falls apart, as it must. If you learn to live in appreciation, you will enter a domain, a vibration that will carry you through the chaos of these times. You will find a type of solace and comfort, and the vibrational rate of your energy body will increase. At some point you will reach what we call escape velocity. You will easily step out of the illusions and the lies of the old world. You will see them for what they are, and you will become a joyous co-creator of a new world that is being birthed even as the old world passes away right before your eyes. But essentially what the Hathors are saying is that appreciation is a specific vibration of consciousness and when we are in that vibration we are elevated."
~ The Hathors through Tom Kenyon, September 22, 2008 Orcas Island, WA, www.tomkenyon.com

A great exercise to practice getting out of negative thinking, into positive thinking that also leads to peace is to write three things you are Grateful for EVERY DAY; morning or night or both—you choose! Do this for 21 days. Research has shown that it takes our brain 21 days to instill a habit. Let's instill a habit of being grateful and thereby receiving more experiences to be grateful for! Whenever I have practiced this it truly lifts me up. There is so much to be grateful for. So many blessings.

I invite you to really count your blessings. Notice the blessings already in your life now. Really take a moment and close your eyes and come into this awareness. Feel the love and gratitude for the beautiful family you have, the shelter over your head, money in your pocket, food in your belly, job you may still have, or the excellent health you and your family may be experiencing and even smaller things that are so big like the smile of your baby when she looks at you. Whatever it is that is in your life, truly see it as the blessing that it is. Gratitude and appreciation are the highest vibration along with love. Although these are external experiences, they can help you come to this state of being within appreciation. The truest and deepest form of appreciation is the appreciation of the present moment in every moment. It comes from deep within. A vortex deep within the opens up that tingles your entire body with energetic awareness of the aliveness of this very moment. Suddenly appreciation, gratitude and love are just there and always have been.

Coming into full awareness of what's already in your life allows more of the SAME to flow your way!

Many master's and guru's state that their only intention when they wake up in the morning is "Thank you". That is an intense feeling when you are present with it. It is so intense Love comes into your awareness with it. Because that is all there is. We only have what is in our present moment. And it is only in the present moment that we can allow the highest good to flow through us. We can feel good now. Not in 10 days or after you've gone through this process or that process, but now. Right now, in this very moment. It's all about your free will and belief that you can be in a higher vibrational good state of being. It's one step, one leap and you are there.

Be grateful for ALL things in your life. Be grateful for the good *and* the "bad". Be grateful and accept that all things are brought to you for your life experience, even the not-so-great stuff. Tell the Universe, THANK YOU for this challenge, this person, or this horrible experience. Then truly feel that gratefulness. As you ask it to show you what lessons it has for you, inspiration comes because you have come to a state of gratitude and acceptance for what IS right now. You realize that all experiences are for your highest and best good. You realize you are timeless. This too shall pass. You are going to get through these experiences without burying them. You are so grateful and happy to have this experience show you what you need to learn about yourself so that you can shine a light on it, integrate the learning's and transmute it into the light being you are! Then suddenly a shift occurs and more wonderful things occur. You come to a state of appreciation, forgiveness, and healing. The shift that occurs within is indescribable. You may only notice little blips on the radar screen at first and then suddenly a ginormous change occurs in that pattern and it stops. You've integrated. You've moved forward. You've evolved. And you can continue to work on the next thing that may come up with living in gratitude and faith. All truly is well.

Love, Love, Love, is the highest vibration there is. Focusing on Love provides you with the essence of who you truly are. As you focus on the Love you see around you, you start to feel it more within you. What you see is what you mirror to the world and what is inside of you. As you emanate love from your entire being you realize we are all love and divine beings. Whatever goes on around you, you know you are connected and come to a state of appreciation for all things. Love is the key. If you only focus on Love that is all you need! Trust that the Divine has it handled. Surrender. Allow what is to be there, no matter what it is because it just Is. The suffering only starts when your mind says a specific challenge "shouldn't" be happening. But it is. So resist the thoughts that say it shouldn't be. It is happening in the present moment. So release the judgments, denials, projections, complaints and whining. Allow it to unfold naturally and it flows through your experience in a much more thorough and expedient way. When you accept what is, you become aware of the something deeper within, that stillness within . . . . peace. It's always there. From this state we can come through any experience.

We can be in our state of peace during any state (such as chaos or anxiety). Just come to a state of allowing what IS in this present moment and suddenly a shift can occur within you. You start to appreciate what *is* even if it's not exactly what you intended for that moment. Just be grateful in that moment and feel inner peace. Or rather be grateful that even if something bad happens we are still able to be at peace inside. We can be in the world but not of it. It's a simple shift in consciousness.

I do my best to check in and ask, "What can I be grateful for in this moment? What is so great and wonderful about right now?" It's not just an appreciation for the people, places, things and experiences in your life, those are external. It goes deeper than that. It's an appreciation for the aliveness that you are. I take deep breaths of awareness and feel the inner peace, my inner beingness pulsating inside of me and all around me. It feels as if it's the energy of the Divine itself. The ultimate connection as we are the Divine.

I feel. I am so grateful for feeling the Divine connection within me. It is this connection that allows me to go forth in this life as it is now. It is the driving force for my entire beingness. It is amazing. It is you and it is me. It is all of us and to feel that connection is a blessed gift. This is my thank you every morning when I wake up.

All we need is Love. I am reminded of two stories of Mother Teresa today. The first is when Mother Teresa was walking towards the building where she was to give a speech. As she neared the building (with many fans milling about) she saw a person lying on the ground. This person was obviously homeless and seemingly hurt but unable to move. Not one person stopped to notice this person on the ground. They just went about their business. Mother Teresa stopped, leaned over and helped the gentlemen up and took him to her home. She did not speak that day. The story is said that he died later that night but not before receiving beautiful kindness from a beautiful stranger. Better to give up a speaking engagement and give a helping hand to a fellow human being. I'd say that is a much more powerful lesson than any speech she might have given that day.

The second story is when Mother Teresa needed to cross enemy lines in the middle of a recent war (to go to a conference, I believe). It was agreed that both sides would stop shooting until Mother Teresa was safely across. So for a brief hour or however long it took no guns were shot, no bombs, nothing. Mother Teresa assisted in stopping a war.

I don't know if I have the strength that Mother Teresa has yet, but if ever there was a person to resonate with, it's Mother

Teresa. If ever there was a worthy goal to strive for, it's this one. It is Love. Mother Teresa offered Love freely and willingly. The Power and Magic of Love goes beyond words. Striving for Love is the highest vibrational frequency we can become.

Take a moment and ask yourself how you can share kindness with others. Start by showing compassion and kindness towards others, instead of inauthentic chatter and faux obviousness to their situation. When you do even one small act of kindness, a mere smile, you feel so radiant inside. It's amazing. Treat all people the same, from the famous and popular to the poor and normal. We truly *are* all the same, so decide to see the light in everyone you come across. Share that positive energy.

As paraphrased from the Dalai Lama on being kind and compassionate: Hatred, self-centered behavior and negative emotions are bad for your health. You are at greater risk for a heart condition if you continue or dwell in those emotions. In contrast a calm Mind, a compassionate mind sustains great health. A positive mental state and mental attitude of warm-heartedness has been proven by science to sustain your health. And I, obviously, agree 100%. Just check in with yourself when you are ill and ask yourself how you were feeling before. There might be emotions of worry, fear or negativity that you felt for a day or a week or months prior to the illness setting in. You truly can make the shift to true inner peace starting right now. The only person you can gain true inner peace from is you.

When you are self-centered, narrow-minded and closed off to the world even seemingly small issues will seem unbearable. However, in contrast, when you are open to all possibilities and let affection in and are open to the world, it is easier to face even the biggest of issues.

Our Divine guidance, our Angels, our Higher Selves are constantly reminding us we *are* Love. We are just now finally removing the blinders from our Spirit. Remember who you are. As you love yourself it is easier to love others. You are love and you are loved. As you flow in the frequency of Love you are in the highest state of peace there is.

Chapter 20

It Just Is

It's not good. It's not bad. It just is.

This is another reminder for you and those you come in contact with. Whenever something happens, good or bad, simply use the phrase "It's not good. It's not bad. It just is." as a mantra. This story that passed down from our ancestors told by Denise Linn during my Soul Coaching training with her, as well as a version by Eckhart Tolle in his book "A New Earth" and by many other mystics is a great story to bring into your conscious awareness. You can share it with your family, friends and clients in their healing of all of life's issues. "It's not good. It's not bad. It just is."

The story goes that a man in a small village found his horse had gotten loose and ran off into the woods. The village people went to his side to console him. Telling him how this was very bad and not good luck. The man told the village people not to fret, for "It's not good. It's not bad. It just is." A few days later the horse comes bounding back with an entire heard of horses! All the village people gathered around amazed! They told him he was right that this was very good luck! The man said, "No, no. It is not good. It is not bad. It just is." The villagers dismissed his comments. Months pass by and then one day the man's son had a terrible accident while training one of the horses. The horse had trampled on his legs and caused him to be permanently unable to walk and in a wheelchair for life. The village people said that this is very bad and not good luck at all. The man again reminds them that this, too, "Is not good. It is not bad. It just is." Of course the village people walked away mumbling what a crazy old man he is. A few more months pass by and a war between villages starts up. Men are being drafted to participate in this war. Most of which are never seen again. The village people go to the man and tell him he was right. His son's injury made it impossible for him to be in the war and he is lucky to have his son alive with him now. The man again says, "It is not good. It is not bad. It just is."

This story is a very important lesson for allowing the Divine to do as it will. There is no attachment to the outcome here. There is no more resistance. Just peace. For, we are reminded that we are here to live life to the fullest and enjoy its ups and downs. We do not need to focus so much on negative happenings or positive happenings but to enjoy the ride. Be in the flow. Take what will come and manifest the best life we can with the art of allowing the surprises of the Universe to occur in its own divine way. We must remember we are Soul's. We are living in a physical body to experience human life. We will survive even death, as we are here to ascend, evolve and progress as we dance our dance with the Divine. We are the Divine experiencing itself!

Chapter 21

Rise Above

Rise Above and Allow Others Their Experience

Letting go is a powerful but necessary self-practice. We must let go, rise above and allow others their experience. Stop caring too much. When we care "too" much about someone else's pain or painful experience we are aligning ourselves into their vibration and resonating at a level that allows us to experience just what they are experiencing. Come to a higher ground, a higher vibrating way of being. Send them love, but allow them to experience what they need to experience. When they are ready they will feel the love we send and the love from the Universe and rise above their experiences. But we must do our best not to relate too closely as we don't want to attract their situation to us. Empathy is helpful to let another know you understand and know where they come from. But we no longer need to care "too" much in order to assist another. Sometimes the best thing we can do is listen and be still. Always remain in your inner peace when around others experiencing something that does not vibrate at our level. Remember, we can be in the world but not of it.

My Husband has nicknamed me his "Spiritual Cheerleader". So I use that name a lot. He says it describes how I am around him and with many people. It's something that comes naturally out in me since my own initial awakening, so I share as I am guided. I share to assist others in empowering themselves to raise their own vibration up. However, sometimes I share when sharing is not asked for or not necessary. Sometimes my Husband just wants to vent and doesn't want to hear how I might be able to assist him. So there is a fine line with my sharing. I must keep myself in check and always ask myself, "Is this a place where I am asked for my advice?" Or, "Is this a place where what I have to share can be of value?" Or, "Is this is place where what I can share is just a sharing because I want to share and is only my ego?" And lastly, "Is this a place where my sharing will even be heard? Is this person ready to even hear me at this time in their evolution?" These are questions I really need to discern within myself often in order to truly remain in a neutral stance, but also a compassionate and selfless stance as a part of my own divine destiny of service.

Sometimes the advice we give someone is simply just our opinion and not right for them. Sometimes the wrong course of action for us may be the right decision for them for wherever they are in their unique experience. It's a path they need to go down even if it's the longer or more challenging path. In the end it's up to them anyway.

The peace that flows through you when you realize that you are actually assisting them and yourself by allowing them to move through their experience is so freeing! You can be there for them in little spurts of compassion when it's right. But not in their face so much they don't even experience the challenge they are meant to go through. We are allowing them to live out their soul's blueprint. This allows them to fully experience what they need to experience from their situation. Their growth is evolving for them in their own way. For many of us, the only way to make a change is to go through an uncomfortable or very challenging life experience. It is these types of energies that push the person to make the necessary changes they were supposed to make at that point in their life.

If we "saved" them with our compassionate ways by alleviating their pain "too soon" then they may not make the change they were supposed to make at that time. All is delayed until they experience something else challenging or uncomfortable to get them to move. This second time may be more painful. That is also how patterns work until we wake up to them and see them for what they are and make a shift. So we are respecting their path as it is laid out perfectly for them. We each experience life differently. It is all perfect. Always see others as the Divine Source connection they are. Our powerful image of them is felt energetically. We do not need to be in their lower vibrating experience anymore. Be the stillness within. Send your love as the highest vibration there is. Be in that love yourself, as this is the only way to truly stay "protected". Since love is the highest vibration there is, this is the place where you keep yourself encompassed. As you emanate this, you are in higher frequencies and are untouchable by anything but love.

When we find ourselves in a situation with someone of lower vibrating energies that we may also feel deep compassion for, take a step back and observe. See where there is an overlapping of merged energy. Ask what is the lesson for you from this experience? What is the mirror for you? Or rather what are you reflecting outwardly that is bouncing back to you now? What is this teaching you? Then remember to bring yourself to a place of love and gratitude for this experience—for this soul before you. Feel the love you have and the love connection you two have with the Divine. Remembering your loving Divine selves and the connection we all have keeps you in the higher vibrating reality of, simply put, love.

Chapter 22

Forgiveness & Acceptance

It's detrimental to our health and our aura and our energy to remain in a state of unforgiveness to anyone for any amount of time. It's absolutely critical to move into a state of forgiveness and stillness. Believe me, I know this and I still work at it with certain people or situations as best I can. So I know and millions out there know what it's like. But it's time . . . not to forgive them for them, but to forgive them for YOU. Forgiveness is for the self, not the other person or situation. It is only to benefit you and your vibration. For your health. For your sanity. For your state of mind. For your energy to be at its optimum best and for you to be the most uplifted highest vibrational you. And it won't happen overnight but at least be open to it. Also, I know that some of us may also start to feel guilty that we are not forgiving someone or something. And hopefully we don't do that because it's counteractive. Guilt is a useless emotion that kills. So now just move away from that thought. Let's move into forgiveness as best we can one step at a time. Breathe it in.

Forgiveness allows you to remove the negative energy blockages that sit within you. If something has angers your or made you upset, you can feel it, process it and release it. But if this same issue is held within you and causes unforgiveness to eat at your soul, you've gone beyond natural emotional processing to being drug down to the depths of victimhood, wallowing and lower negative vibrational frequencies. It is prudent that we not let those past or present issues eat at our inner peace anymore. We do no need to contribute to the mass consciousness by dwelling, staying in victim mode and being unable to forgive. You can forgive! And we do not need to feel the need to control another's behavior. There is no need to be in that lower vibration anymore. We can only control our own choices and our own peaceful state.

Not everyone will be completely happy and at peace all at the same time; at least not yet. But that doesn't mean you have to wait until they are in order to be happy and at peace yourself. We also do not need to take the negative bait and feel whatever it is that another is feeling or wanting us to feel for their own unconscious self-centered desires. We do not need to react to a situation with negativity anymore. We can process our emotions healthily but they do not need to rule us in a negative fashion. We do not have to respond in anger to another no matter what poor behavior they are showing us. This is allowing the negative monster in to your energy body.

Most of us have probably been on both ends of this stick. We've gotten angry over something and expected a friend or loved one to react with anger or to also be in a state of anger (aka resistance or disconnection) with us. However, it didn't seem to happen as you expected or have seen in times past. They weren't angry and simply took a stance of letting it go. We probably got angrier over this and fumed. But when the angry negative monster finally passed and you reviewed how this situation got out of control and reviewed your friend's non-reaction, you realized they might have had it more together than you did. What's their secret!? Granted sometimes the reaction you didn't see from another was happening on the inside instead and they were processing in that fashion. Or they were possibly in a state of denial and repressing emotions that wanted to be released in healthy ways. So for them it will take a bit longer to learn how to release emotions healthily. And lastly, they could have been taking higher ground as I discuss here and letting the issue go.

It's best to take a deep breath, let it roll off your back at times and remain very present in every moment. Especially in moments like these that might draw you to react rather than be in your inner peace and coming from a state of love. Don't let another person or situation drag you down. Use the power of your very own will and tell yourself it's not personal. It's the game of life. A nice inner visual is to become transparent (this amazing idea inspired by Eckhart Tolle). Instead of resisting and being a wall, be transparent and let the negative reactions flow through you. Breathe in and out. Be aware of the breath. Be with the negative energy and allow it to be there. Feel what it feels like completely. See what is there. Then let it flow out naturally. Allow the emotion or issue to flow in and then out, as if passing right on through. Let it go. You are no longer a sticky lower density match for that negativity and it doesn't even need to stick around. The energy dissipates or moves on in your presence. Balance remains and a new purpose or way of living arises. The shift you feel inside when you stop reacting and come from a state of love is amazing!

Even the small moments can build up if you don't change your mind thoughts and energy. If someone cut you off while you were driving, quickly send them feelings of forgiveness and love if you've immediately gotten upset and sent out negative energies to that person. If you are impatient at a long line don't send out negative thoughts to the people in line or the cashier working feverishly to get through the line. Instead, take a deep breath. Close your eyes. Breathe in and out. Sometimes simply breathing releases the claustrophobic energy. Know it is all Divine. You know not why this is occurring but it is occurring for a reason. I like to take mini-meditation trips while waiting in lines. It is crucial that you not build up these occurrences. You build up more unnecessary karma that will come back around to haunt you immediately or very soon. A negative spiral ensues, unless you stop yourself in your tracks and send love to those beautiful Divine strangers. What is good about this situation? These strangers are showing you what you are mirroring right now with your energy. So send them love and thanks. I like to visualize a surprising serene face on the stranger as they receive unconditionally loving rose petals or golden stars. Think happy. Think love. Share that and it comes back to you.

I know this stance is more of a challenge for those you love and hold so dear. But it is necessary for your soul and theirs that you connect and reach the peaceful state no matter what is going on around you. Not to mention you are of no use to anyone if you are not in your divine connection from within. You are joining the masses and promoting disconnection when you condemn another. Aligning with acceptance, love, appreciation and looking for the positive side of things allows peace to flood in. In fact, if you remain in a peaceful state, you are actually helping them MORE by being in that peaceful state. It is only when you are in that completely neutrally peaceful higher vibrational place that you can assist in raising another vibration with your contributions. Just by being around you they will match your stronger vibration and shift into a higher way of being. Sometimes immediately! So by forgiving, accepting and aligning your frequency with inner peace you are contributing to more positive experiences and more inner peace in your life and the lives of those you come in contact with. Remember, what you focus on expands.

If I let the fact that my ex-Husband owes me over seven grand in back child support get to me (and I have let it get to me at times) I would never be at peace within myself. I am learning just as we all are. I've followed guidance and justice is working itself out as it is meant to happen. I remind myself that the Universe supports me in all ways always. I am seeing each role as divine and allowing, as much as possible, what will be to be. While in court this last time, I decided not to have a set intention other than for the highest and best, good of all. Right there while talking with the Judge I simply saw the divine spark within him and also in my ex-Husband. The divine spark I saw comes to the surface and flows out. This brings me such inner peace myself. I connect with the Divine in all beings. We are all deserving of divine love and connection, even to those who have attacked you in any way, shape or form. Remember all are deserving of this love and know the divine resides within us all. Only connect with that part of them—the truest part of them.

As I am in a state of peace my vibration is unaffected by lower vibrations. So right there feeling so peaceful and okay with whatever happens next, I am in an accepting yet allowing state. Whatever will be, will be and I am okay with it. So what happened next shocked me. Instead of simply giving my ex-Husband more time to work on his issues, the Judge didn't like his responses (the truth of him came out at that moment) and he threw him in jail for 30 days. I was flabbergasted, but then reminded that it is all divine. It apparently was meant to be for my ex-Husband's divine plan in order for him to reach closer to waking up. From then on his child support responsibility has been paid. Sometimes it's late but always catching up pretty fast. So it seems that this divine occurrence has worked for justice of the highest and best, good of all.

Sometimes we are guided to sit still with a situation. Sometimes we are guided to move away or leave a situation. Sometimes we are guided to use righteous action for positive change. Each person and situation is unique. For me this situation called for righteous action and seeing the Divine in everyone while remaining in my peaceful center. Go with how you are guided. From this I am still learning the art of forgiveness, acceptance and letting go.

The learning curve is different for each of us. Sometimes I need a reminder or two or twenty. 9 A reminder that we are all Divine and all aspects of the Divine. We are here playing roles. The main goal is to awaken to the unconscious sleep we've allowed for so long. Not everyone is there. And many are there but are still working towards this goal that may take lifetimes. We must simply thank the situation for what it is. Ask your guidance if there are any lessons to be learned by you and process it. And even in processing we can be in our inner peace. Simply reach in there to your inner fire and bring it forth. The power is within you.

Forgiveness is a willingness to see that we are all one. We are the one who created the act that happened to us, as much as we are the person it happened to. Embracing the Oneness connection of all of us takes away the separation and opens us up to true love. Albert Einstein states, "A human being is a part of a whole, called by us a 'universe' a part limited in time and space. He experiences himself, his thoughts and feelings as something separated from the rest . . . a kind of optical delusion of his consciousness. This delusion is a kind of prison for us, restricting us to our personal desires and to affection for a few persons nearest to us. Our task must be to free ourselves from this prison by widening our circle of compassion to embrace all living creatures and the whole of nature in its beauty."

You can simple allow whatever it is to be as it is in its <u>own space</u> (no longer affecting yours) and accept that it is what it is, while checking in with your divine connection. Bring your vibrations higher as you connect. Feel thoughts and emotions of inner peace. Use the strong abilities of the mind to bring you there by imagining a forgiving moment, or by imagining yourself feeling the forgiveness, acceptance and imminent serenity. Just breathe. Remind yourself that YOU have the power to be in whatever vibration you choose. It's up to you. It's your free will choice! Whatever it takes to get you to a good space will take you out of that negative space to a higher freer bliss space. You may use prayer. You may use energy healing. You may use yoga. You may use thoughts of your children and other loved ones. You may use mudras, mantras, meditation, breathwork or funny flicks to get you there. Sometimes you are able to just remind yourself of inner peace and you are there right now! Whatever gets you there immediately will work! Make a funny face at yourself in the mirror. Trust me, even when you are very mad it causes a positive shift in your subconscious and you feel yourself start to soften. Peace is coming. Peace is here. The blissful state is within you. It's always there for you to bring into your awareness. It's your choice.

Chapter 23

Mirrors—Conscious Awareness

"Better to light a candle than to curse the darkness."
~ Chinese Proverb, Bertrand Russell, Unpopular Essays

F ind your mirrors. Become aware and release your mirrors. Start noticing the mirrors around you in your life; from the big things to the little things. Remember everything we see in our lives—EVERYTHING—we attract to ourselves. Nothing is random. We can choose to see the messages in everything we see or not.

If you get angry or frustrated over something, then this is a mirror you need to recognize. If you react to something it is something you need to look at. This is a part of our shadow selves that we must see. We can't ignore the things that aggravate us and wish them away. We must first become aware of them, see what lessons we needed to see in them (some might call Karma), and only then integrate them for transmutation into pure life. Little by little we can recognize and integrate our shadow selves into ourselves, and little by little raise our awareness and our vibrations. We can however, see the positive in everything as well and thereby raising its vibration to a higher good, a higher awareness and appreciate all those mirrors! As you appreciate and feel gratitude for the lessons they integrate even faster, seemingly easier and you are in an inner peace. Know that even while doing this work you can be in inner peace in that moment as well. They can co-exist.

The mirror is something to become very consciously aware of. As you will notice, the mirror contains your life experiences being shown to you or rather reflected back to you. Our "Shadow" will show up in these mirrored experiences of ours. We learn from the "Shadow" experiences and transmute those mirrored lessons. (I go deeper about our "Shadows" in Book Two *Divine Embrace*).

For example, why did you suddenly get impatient when your child interrupted you while trying to clean the house? This is a simple example. Let's say your answer is that you knew later you would not have the energy to get this done, so you wanted to do it as fast as possible. Any interruption might delay that and ruin the mode you are in. So there is an unfounded fear that time will run out. There are also unconscious things going on, behind the scenes if you will, to become aware of over time. Maybe this is something engrained in you since childhood as was taught to you by your parents too. Maybe there are more insights that come to the surface as you neutrally (like a child) examine your reactions and the why's and fears behind them. But you might be missing out on an opportunity to show kindness and compassion with patience to your child, even in the midst of cleaning house. You might miss out on a beautiful moment. Don't get me wrong, when you say you need to finish cleaning they need to respect that time too, but there is a kind way (even kind in a stern fashion) to handle the situation rather than abrupt impatience. And during these moments you can just allow what will be to be, and still remain in your center, in your connection to source and in your inner peace.

Release the pent up emotions of anger, loneliness, sadness, jealousy, hatred, unforgiveness, fear, and the list goes on. As your Kundalini awakens, more "stuff" will come up. It is your job to allow this to flow through you and release it. Don't resist it. Surrender. Just allow it to be. Be in these emotions and realize that the so called negative ones are a mirror of something within you that you are now ready to face and release. Suddenly you realize these feelings go away faster and more peace than you can imagine remains.

It is awesome to know that when you align with an even greater path for yourself, with even greater desires for the end results, how the Universe just meets your every need. There is a form of knowing what you want and becoming one with that result, while still surrendering to the outcome. We are supported by the Universe in all ways, always! This is a great reminder to not let fear get in the way of what we want because fear is nothing but what we feed it. We can sit with it, be in it and it will dissipate and dissolve, transmuting into pure energy!

Becoming conscious of every moment and remaining in your inner peace is becoming aware of any mirrors that come up and allowing them to surface for release. There may be forgiveness that needs to happen on your part to others and on your part to yourself. Just allow rather than burying them. Burying them only allows them to fester and surface in larger ways to get you to take notice of them. See patterns that show up and realize these are patterns to also become aware of and release. Patterns such as attracting the same type of partner in your life; for example, attracting an alcoholic as your partner or an abusive person. Whatever the pattern is, become aware of it. Ask yourself what lessons there are for you to attract such a person. Is there something in your deep past of your childhood that brought this pattern up. Maybe it's a lesson you need to learn. Maybe it's attached to past lives where even going under hypnosis might help you. Just take what insights come to you personally and know that your Soul knows the truth and you will release this. Becoming aware of it is the first step. Allowing for forgiveness and release the second. Then it naturally integrates and transforms you into a higher being. More of your true divine self flows out!

No matter what, your lessons are your lessons. You will face them eventually. As I like to say, listen to the whispers or you will have no choice but to hear the screams. Akira Dawn of LovesGuidingLight.com sent out a 'Daily Spark' with the perfect message of looking within: "When our buttons are pushed our first impulse is to react—and usually in a big way. After all, that's what those defenses were put there for in the first place! To cover up that tender spot and keep it safe! If we're aware enough to not react . . . awesome. If we're not, that's fine, too, because either way at some point along the line we'll get the invaluable chance to become aware, and take a look at what's being triggered. To not point outside of ourselves . . . to instead take the time to take a look inside—this takes guts. And it is also one of the greatest opportunities for healing and personal growth that we can encounter. Be gentle with yourself. It's scary! But it's so worth it. :) *hugs!*"

When you wake up to the moments of the Shadow self being reflected back to you it is that much easier to face the challenges rather than repress them. When you repress them they grow bigger and bigger. Dr. Carl Jung agrees when he says, "Good does not become better by being exaggerated, but worse, and a small evil becomes a big one through being disregarded and repressed. The shadow is very much a part of human nature, and it is only at night that no shadows exist."

As you become aware of the ego moments, you are shining the light on the shadow or darkness. As you do this, it dissolves into nothing. You transmute. You transform. More and more! Keep it up!

The Mirror of All That Is: I find that when I remember that no matter what happens to me or around me, my Divine Self, my inner spark, that special place within me remains untouched. I am the Divine and as I remember that, my light spreads. As I remember this in times of strife or trouble, I come back to myself, my center. I realize it's always there . . . the Divine. I am always okay. I am always Divine. And I can choose to spread this around and reflect something back to myself that is more pleasing or simply first allow what is, see what lessons may be there, but not be *of* the experiences, just the observer (in Divine Light always).

Chapter 24

Choice & Reactions

Choice

You choose in every moment how you're going to feel. You can let that moment take your power away or you can keep you power and be grateful and happy for every moment. No matter what is happening around you, you have choice. We have free will. We can choose to be happy, blissful, peaceful or the opposite. The two base options here are we can simply choose love or fear. It's your choice.

For example, my husband wanted to take a peaceful shower but our one-and-a-half year old kept opening the door and playing, which kept interrupting his mode of feeling and also got the room colder. Instead of getting angry or frustrated, he chose in that moment to think of how cute she was being and be grateful for her and her presence. That is a very simple yet profound example of how in every moment no matter what is happening we have the choice in how we feel!

Likewise you can wake up every day and say, "YES!" to the day. You can choose that today (and everyday) are beautiful wonderful days and you can make it work out that way just be setting the tone in your own energy. Just feel wonderful, even if you're waking up tired. Forget about all that other stuff from lack of sleep to the prior night or prior days that may have weighed heavy on you. Just forget it all. When you wake up, shift your energy. Jump up and say, "YES!" to life right now! As you do this you *will* see positive profound results.

I am doing little things to come back to my center and no longer multi-task as much as possible. Multi-tasking does have its benefits when necessary but for the most part I am working on living in the Now. I am working on no longer doing more than one thing at a time, but enjoying the juiciness of the present moment of one activity at a time. For instance, I am doing my best not to use my cell phone while driving. Not only a dangerous distraction, but if it's not an emergency it can wait. I have a 15-20 minutes driving time till I pick up my kids. So I am choosing those few minutes of blissfully driving and breathing, while listening to good music when I am drawn to it. I don't listen to the news either. That takes me away from the experience and also since most of it is negative it is a useless pull on our vibration. So I blissfully drive. You can do this while doing the dishes, the laundry, and bath time with the kids, etc. Simply enjoy the moment as it is. I am choosing to stay true to my spiritual center. I am choosing these new ways of being to bring me back to my true divine connection.

In every moment there is a choice. You choose the joyful circumstances that surround you now. And you choose the not-so-happy circumstances that may surround you in every moment. Every time you start to believe or feel something you are making a choice. You are choosing a vibration. You can choose to let that person who cut you off in line make you upset and lower your vibration. Or you can choose to let it go. You can choose to come up with a story within yourself about that person that will keep your vibration high, like maybe they were in a rush to get to work as they are late. Or maybe that person cut you off on the road because their wife is about to have a baby. Or maybe that person's clothes you judged as dirty and old are the only clothes that person can afford to wear. You choose how you view a situation. And most importantly you choose when NOT to view aka judge a situation in any form. This is the highest level of being. Choose not to know. Choose to simply be in your higher vibration no matter what. It's not good. It's not bad. It just is.

The dominating vibration will be the "winning" vibration. That means if you are totally within your peace and bliss and vibrating at one with this, any outside source will not move you from this frequency. In fact, you will affect the other frequency that was there in either the person or place. This means if you see someone come into a room and they are flippant and angry and want to lash out at anyone in their path, and if you are not holding strong in your peace state, you may become susceptible to their shift in frequency and also become angry. In every moment there is a choice. Hold strong to your peaceful vibration.

Reactions

I'd like to address negativity and our reactions to it now. Believe it or not, most negativity does not come from malicious conscious intent by another. Most negativity comes from our reactions whether conscious or unconscious to another's actions (be it self-centered actions or simply obliviousness). Eckhart Tolle has this one licked when he said, "Every time you react to something there is a strengthening of your form identity; the psychological sense of me." Even when you hear something said and think 'no you're wrong and I am right', there is a self seeking there and it is your ego speaking. Eckhart Tolle explains further, "Whatever form arises, it could be a thought that comes in or an emotion that goes through you. See that it is not resisted but it is allowed. It's allowed . . . mmm and there it is. Allowed means that you are no longer a reactive entity. It doesn't mean that you can't respond but response is action that arises that is totally right for this situation but it doesn't come unless you first say yes [allow] and then there it is." Many of us are too attached to what others are doing and saying. It's time to let go. Our truth does not have to rely upon another and what they have to say. It's time to feel the divine from within and emulate that out to the world no matter what another is doing or saying.

Sometimes our reactions are towards another's simply living in their truth. Someone else's truth might not match our own and that might cause us to resist them or the lesson it is reflecting to us. Sometimes someone is simply acting as they always would but when we see it our reaction to it is very negative. We might lash out at them in a negative way. To them they don't see the reasons why. They don't see it because they are not being negative. And if they are unawake they will also react poorly back and a negative spiral occurs because we reacted badly to a situation. A situation that could have been resolved with our own INTERNAL work. A situation that could have been worked through with kindness no matter what the other person was doing or saying.

Sometimes we can communicate and work through the issues while remaining in our blissful state. Sometimes by putting ourselves in another's shoes we can see how and why they could do whatever it is they did. Sometimes understanding doesn't come so easily. What if I don't understand or comprehend why they are doing something? What if I never do? It doesn't matter. We must strive to come to a place of not knowing and not caring. Not caring is meant in a state of neutrality. And it is a great practice to trick yourself and think the best of someone and know that whatever their reasons they are divine. We each are experiencing this life in our own unique way and we each have our own trials and tribulations to work through as our lessons in life. And we each will express this differently. Tell yourself it's okay. Take a step back from reacting unconsciously and start to first check in with the Self. Breathe deeply before reacting. And remain in a grounding, centered state of Being. Your reaction is yours, not theirs, to deal with. Don't play the game of drama anymore and contribute negatively. The karma (action of reacting positively or negatively) keeps you going in circles. (That is until we transcend karma; realizing our Divine Self.)

A fun example is the road rage example. Such as reacting to another's slow driving or another person cutting us off. Maybe they didn't see us. But that option doesn't stop us from honking our horn and yelling our heads off. Not that they can hear us. Sometimes the reaction stems from the fear of a possible accident. Other times we are in a rush and are impatient due to our own ineffective scheduling to drive in peace. And sometimes we are already angry or upset over another issue and this one thing compounds the issue and suddenly a mega fume of heat and negativity is released.

We can do something about this. We can coherently drive in peace and harmony. We can live amongst others in peace. We can do our best to stick to a schedule, not booking things we definitely cannot make or living in our truth and telling others there's no way you can make it there in time without driving unsafely and not in harmony and peace. If we have all the time in the world and we're still getting angry and out of our peaceful place while driving, then check in with yourself. Ask yourself, why are you in a rush now? Why are you getting angry at everyone else when you don't need to? Check in and see if there is something else that is bothering you. And if you already know what it is, pull over. Take a deep breath and let out the emotions you have been repressing and are now spewing all over the road at all the innocent passers by. Let it go. It's time to feel good. You are allowed to feel good. It is your RIGHT in this life now to feel good about yourself and your life. If there is something that needs to be done, make a note to go do it in divine timing. Make a promise to yourself that you can be in this world happy, that you will consciously check in and always release your emotions as immediately as they come to you in healthy ways. So as not to spread your unconscious negativity to others.

It is helpful to give you another example here. Let's say you're a parent and your child is acting up big time. You've done all you can do: timeouts, grounding, and it still occurs. What are you to do? Yell? Get angry inside yourself causing much internal turmoil? Or simply know you are being consistent and staying your center. And, let's say, after all this your child goes to bed almost every night upset, whining and crying because you turned the TV off at their bedtime. You have to tell them it's bedtime and to go to sleep. It upsets you dearly that you have to say good night to your child upset every night instead of happy and lovingly. During some of these occasions you might be able to easily handle the situation and let it roll off your back. Other times it upsets you to no end and you angrily yell at them about how you'd like them to go to bed happy and for both of you to hug and kiss goodnight in harmony. Now, the yelling only compounded the issue making it worse and you are blaming the child for their feelings. It's true, discipline shall still occur but we can do it as kindly, but sternly in our power, as possible.

We're here to guide them, not persecute them for their wrong doings. All the while remembering our children are also our mirrors for ourselves, so keep watch as to what it means to you and what is inside of you. As their guide we can discipline in harmony. You can tell them your feelings but do it in a compassionate way and stick with your rules. They may still get upset but you've discharged your poor reaction. You still have to deal with the fact that you are upset about how they are going to bed, but they do not need to receive your angry yelling. It's a negativity fueled charge that you aim at them. Instead walk away and talk with your partner, your friend or your guides. Breathe. Let it out. Scream into a pillow and cry your head off till it is released. This is your own private release that doesn't send negativity to the child. Instead it dissolves within you. Anger begets anger. And harmony begets harmony. It's a strong lesson for me over and over again. So we must strive to be in harmony and awareness with ourselves and our children. Your peaceful vibration will win if it is the dominating vibration.

They are allowed their reactions. Each person is allowed their reaction. Let's say you have something unpleasant to say to someone but it is within your truth and you do it with kindness. They react in a way that is unexpected by you. But you remain in your center. You remain in your peace. You ALLOW that person their divine reaction, no matter what it is. And you walk away both living in your truths. And remember it is always OUR CHOICE to react or not react to a situation. It is always our Free Will to live in peace now.

Some days more than others we may be feeling more low on the totem pole than usually and other days we are flying high. So there are some days where we truly need to make a conscious effort big time to surround ourselves with positive affirmations, positive people, uplifting meditations, inspirational exercise, positive awareness of our thoughts and being. Rejuvenating our energies can happen with visualizations of positive experiences to visualizations of golden beautiful energy beaming down to you and to the depths of your soul. You can feel rejuvenated, refreshed and invigorated as you keep on it!

Mike George founder of *www.Relax7.com* shares a beautiful way to transform negativity, "First, do not absorb it—don't be an emotional sponge. Second do not reflect it back. Otherwise you begin a cycle of emotional exchanges which may last a long time. And third, do the one thing which marks us as intelligent human beings—transform it. Even if the scene is a disaster there is some benefit somewhere in it. Even if you are watching two peoples beliefs or opinions slug it out to the edge of violence, don't take sides. Instead offer a solution then stand well back. Even if the person hates you, accept their state of being and return the light of love. In time, with patience, it will illuminate their darkness, and return to you by the bucketful! Just wait."

As told in the *Bhagavad Gita: A Walkthrough for Westerners* by Jack Hawley, "The serene person who is absorbed in God, living thus in peace, is the true renunciate. Maintaining an even mind in heat and cold, pleasure and pain, honor and disgrace marks the spiritually mature. Maintaining physical, mental, and intellectual balance no matter how difficult the challenge leads to permanent cheerfulness, which is the sure sign of a yogi." We will all get there in our own time. We can live life consciously. We can strive to become conscious of our reactions. Be the witness. Simply observe as if outside of yourself. Come back to yourself with peace being your constant state of awareness. We can re-act with kindness when we remain in our center knowing that we are ALL divine light beings of God. We are each living in our truths. We are each expressing our divine selves. Our dance in this life is our unique expression of the divine through us. It is all Divine. And remember my favorite mantra: It's not good. It's not bad. It just is.

Chapter 25

What you Focus Upon Expands

The Universe will always comply and prove you right no matter what you believe. So it's helpful to truly believe the best in people and situations. Focus on the good. Do not focus on the bad. Yes, we must face our shadow selves. The idea is not to dwell there. Just realize it, see it, learn from it and integrate it into your Light self. Your vibrations rise as you allow, accept, receive (be receptive) and transmute into pure light. As you become aware of the ego moments, you are shining the light on the shadow or darkness. As you do this, it dissolves into nothing. You transmute. You transform. More and more! Keep it up!

Realize your emotions. Release your emotions as they come up. If you are angry, be angry and allow it to be released healthily. If you are sad, cry and talk it out. If you are happy be happy. Really show it. Who said you can't smile when you feel happy? Who was the person that said we need to be stone-faced when walking by people even if we are so very happy in that moment!? Even if it's more "politically correct" to politely nod your head and say hello. Why not smile instead! Or even just random laughter because you remembered a funny moment or something beautiful just occurred to you. Feel it, live it and be it now. Now is all we have anyway.

Fact: Emotions are addictive. There are receptors in our chemistry that fire off when we feel an emotion. (As illustrated in the movie *What the Bleep Do We Know!?*) And they attract more of those same receptors and therefore emit energy out to the Universe by Law of Attraction to receive more of the experiences that attract more of that emotion. You can choose which ones to shift to. A shift in consciousness is all it takes. I choose happier emotions, so happier experiences are drawn to me most of the time in order to produce that happy emotion. And even when they're not happy experiences I do my dandiest to be blissful, peaceful and happy while working through issues healthily.

There are challenges. We are human and as long as I stay in my happy emotion, easily allowing the emotions to exist (rather than festering) and release whatever emotions may come up in the *now* then more happy experiences come and the challenges are easier to face. We can remain in our peace while being in challenging moments. Just be in the space of the emotion you desire. Even better, just be in your center. Feel your Divine self. Remember your divine self. As you are in that peaceful state magical elements transpire for whatever challenge you are facing. The challenge does not become as "challenging". It withers away smoothly. So it flows in and just as fast as it came in, it flows out. The way it's supposed to be naturally.

Perception is key. Believe the best in people, not for *their* sake, but for *yours*. Keep yourself in a higher vibration and change your thoughts and feelings towards another for something more positive. Make that shift. Since we are all One, what you see in another is in you. Believing the best in people assists you in raising your frequency to much higher states of being. We can change our concept of life-changing events or people from negative to positive. We can change the way they feel to us. As we take responsibility for these occurrences by accepting them as our highest and best good, we more easily move into forgiveness and release. We release any negative hold they may have had on us. We can change our perception about a person or situation just by our mere wanting to.

Even the Dalai Lama says in times of tragedy, sorrow and sadness you need to look for the positive side of things within it. The Dalai Lama shares with us to believe in God, the Creator. To know that the All-knowing must have some reason for the experiences you are going through. I recently attended a gathering where I was blessed to see the Dalai Lama and he spoke of this with regards to any tragedy or experience. We can reflect on his being exiled from his own country and knowing even then he must have practiced the art of positive thinking, searching for the positive angle. I know there are many positive angles to his being exiled. His being out here in the world allows us to have even more exposure to such a religion and culture that we might not have been as exposed to if this wrong-doing did not occur. He's been gone now for fifty years and he still practices non-violence with the hope that someday Tibet will be free again. His vibrational frequency is a blessing to us all. Not to mention that he is just such a sweet dear man! As he reminded us during his talk, in Buddhism they have a saying, "Hope for the best and prepare for the worst." If the worst thing has happened it is not so bad because you've taken the time to prepare. And if it does you can then implore the act of positive angles on the situation. Know that everything happens for a reason and there is truly a positive outcome from the events.

I was watching a Charmed episode the other night where its theme was: "See no evil, hear no evil, speak no evil". It's one I have seen a few times, but the show still fascinates me. This particular episode was the one with the three monkey's who had temporarily had some of the Charmed Ones abilities. After ridding the monkey's of those abilities, Pheobe, (charmed with the ability of premonitions—telling the future) asked the three monkey's to show Piper and Pru what they thought of evil. One by one each monkey's hands rose up. One monkey's hands covered his eyes, the second monkey's hands covered his ears and the third monkey's hands covered his mouth.

I've heard this saying a hundred times but it just clicked with me on an even higher level. No doubt many others have come to this same epiphany I am about to share with you. The saying, "See no evil, Hear no evil, Speak no evil" has been seen with the picture of three monkey's doing just as they did in the above Charmed episode. This saying has been said to be of people who don't want to be involved.

R. Brash in *How Did It Begin: A fascinating study of the superstitions, customs, and strange habits that influence our daily lives* explains, "It [the picture of the monkey's] dates back to at least the 7th century and is part of the teaching of the Vadjra cult that if we do not hear, see or talk evil, we ourselves shall be spared all evil." (Pocket Book, New York, 1969)

In its obvious terms, the meaning is of looking the other way and evil will not be in the vicinity of you. This goes beyond turning the other cheek or ignoring something evil that is so blatantly in front of you. The deeper level is that anything negative is evil. So we can transpose these words. I have a strong belief that the more negative you are the more negativity comes your way. Much of my own experiences alone tell me this is true. Vice versa is also true. The more positive you are, the more positivity will come your way.

The more you focus on something, the stronger you put out vibrations/energy on whatever it is you are focusing on. So if you are focusing on something negative that happened to you at the start of a day and you keep remembering, picturing and feeling those negative feelings from that one moment or experience in the start of the day, the more you are putting out those vibes/energies to receive MORE of that experience. You are TELLING the Universe to bring you MORE of what you are focusing on!!! And there is no surprise when more negative things occur from this frame of focus.

So let's say you start your day out awesome, the sun is shining and all goes smoothly on your way in to work. You are focused on remembering that sunrise you were able to enjoy as you rode in to work. To top it all off your favorite song came on the radio—at the beginning no less! More good news comes to you about an issue you had had yesterday, however, it's been resolved easily—probably without you even having to lift a finger. Your loan goes through, you and your children are at peace and harmony with each other all day, you are in the best, most happiest and peaceful mood you have ever been in. How wonderful are these days!

It seems like you just kept focusing and remembering those happy moments, and it spiraled into more wonderful happy moments filled with miracles throughout your day! These days happen and they do happen everyday. If you believe it! There may be "challenges" along the way. That's why we're here. But we must focus on positive outcomes, positive solutions and only positive happenings. Unless, of course, you prefer being miserable.

Sometime these awesome days go by without another thought. We take these wonderful peaceful days for granted as just regular days. Instead we can take these happy positive moments and turn them into more happy positive moments JUST by focusing on them. Feel the gratitude of those days and focus on being happy in the moment and knowing more is coming as you become open to all positive possibilities.

As for me, I prefer my happy, loving, peaceful, harmonious sense of well-being I have most of the time! I strive for all of the time! I don't watch the news, I avoid negative radio talk and (as much as I can) negative TV shows and movies. A challenge for me has been to rid myself of negative music. The tune may even be pleasant, however, the words or phrases denote something negative happening or about to happen and I don't want to attract that type of situation to myself, so even though I love the tune, I must turn the station. This is the same for negative people and situations in my life. I steer clear of all negative issues that I can and work through any others with positive focus and positive energy.

I can tell you this, this positive outlook I have now wasn't always there and because of that, my life wasn't always as happy as it could have been. Now that I focus on my happy moments, release what needs to be released when there is a need, I receive what I focus on. I choose positive situations in my life. That is my focus.

"See no evil, hear no evil, speak no evil" takes on new meaning for me as I evolve and I do hope that this brings more clarity and positive happenings for you too!

Nothing has power over you unless you focus on it and allow it. It's all about your intention.

By shifting your perception to something more positive, you shift your vibration. Your frequency is changing! It can happen in an instant if you believe it or over a slow progression. But it does happen if you consciously set yourself up to change it! Do this in every moment of your life. You can wake up and say "YES" to life every day. It's in our waking moments that our daily life is set up. Take these moments and feel a GREAT day, a day of splendor, peace, and joy! As you do this consciously every day magic occurs in your life. Shift your focus and expand it into the positive perceptions.

Align Your Vision

A powerful way for me to stay in my Peace is to visualize. The energy transmits as you enter the world of visualization. Your feeling is a compass to where you are resonating. We each have a frequency that we uniquely vibrate in. It is our unique finger print for the soul. So if you become more consciously aware of how you are feeling, you will then be able to shift that feeling if it's not a feeling you desire. So do whatever it takes to feel Peace, if that is your desire. I regularly make use of two visualization methods to attain my desire of inner peace and bliss (or anything else I desire).

I am a big fan of visualizing colorful energies cleansing me. This act of visualizing these beautiful focal points brings to me a divine connection to Source. Oh what a feeling. The first method is where I visualize energy in colors surrounding me throughout and within; where I, basically, AM energy. We are energy beings so this actually is not a stretch here. It has been found that many who visualize certain colors for certain ailments will assist in their own physical healing (as well as mental, emotional, and spiritual healing). And can utilize breathwork while visualizing colors to assist in healing. A major portion of the Divine Embrace process is visualizing and/or feeling energy in colors and vibration. Truly feeling the visual as if it's happening in the Now is key because it IS happening in the Now.

My morning ritual starts with me standing in mountain pose (yoga asana where you stand up, spine straight, head lifted as if the crown is reaching for the ceiling and arms straight at your sides with arms and legs activated). I will then visualize the Violet Flame of St. Germaine, pink unconditional love energy, then blue-white sparkling angelic energy, then gold light energy, and finally God's white light energy sealing me. I take my time feeling each of these colors and vibrations. This brings me back to my Divine Energy Self. I do this daily with my grounding and other daily energy practices as my morning ritual. I also do this many times throughout the day. The energy I visualize brings me back to my true self. I feel the energy being that I am when I am visualizing. In essence, I am aligning with my energy body and Higher Self and activating it from within. This is powerful for me to do in getting to my inner peace. Everyone can do this. For others that are not so visual, it may be a feeling you intentionally try to feel instead. Do what feels right for you always.

A second way to visualize is to visualize and truly feel yourself in the feeling of peace (or of anything you desire, but here we are working with inner peace). If that requires picturing a beautiful serene piece of nature (an ocean, deep in serene woodland, a secluded lake, etc.) then do it. As Wayne Dyer said, "Contemplate your self being surrounding by the conditions you wish to produce." Whatever it takes for you to be in that place in the present moment is what you should do. We are all unique, so we will all find unique ways to reach the same feeling. All paths lead to the same. So see it, feel it, BE it! By the Law of Attraction it is so! This means that if you are imagining a positive experience and truly in the depths of that experience, you are in the feeling state of that experience and therefore vibrating at the frequency of the positive experience, which then sends out a signal, like a beacon to the Universe, to send you more of that feeling-state, more of that frequency you are in at that moment. So it goes without saying that you want to consciously try to be in that state as often as possible (by way of manifesting through visualizing or any number of other manifesting methods) of what you so desire, to feel that state and focus on receiving new experiences that brings on this feeling.

A great historical example is recited by Catherine Ponder on her website www.CatherinePonder.wwwhubs.com, "One must first image or conceive it. The image makes the condition. Without the image there can be no condition. The French doctor, Emile Coue, proved the healing power of the imagination at the turn of the Century. After more conventional methods of treatment had failed, people from all over Europe sought out Dr. Coue for healing. The success of his cures became so widespread that at his height, he treated as many as one hundred people a day.

"His method? He deliberately set up the picture of healing in each patient's mind by first assuring him, 'Nobody ought to be sick!' Dr. Coue then persisted in making that mental picture firm in the patient's mind by having him affirm daily, 'Every day in every way I am getting better and better.'

"This Frenchman taught that the subconscious mind, which controls the body, was most quickly impressed by mental pictures. By changing those mental pictures, one could quickly change the subconscious, and consequently the body which houses it. He proved that the imagination is a much stronger force than the will; that when the imagination and will are in conflict, the imagination can always triumph.

"Thus, if your imagination is picturing health, it is possible for that health to manifest in your body, regardless of a diagnosis to the contrary or a previous history of ill health. Knowing this, you should deliberately picture yourself as whole and well. The reasoning power of your will may insist that you cannot be healed, but pay it no attention. If you will dare to picture health consistently anyway, then your imagination is free to work for you to produce that health. Whatever the mind pictures and expects, that it will also build and produce for you!"

Chapter 26

Love Is All There Is

Remember the Divine Within

Remember your divine connection. Remember you are Light, always have been and always will be. Feel this divine essence within yourself every day and even several times a day when you may forget. Come back to this remembrance. And, also, remember the divine connection you have with all beings. We are ALL connected. Not just the people that are beloved, not just the people in your family, not just your friends, not just at key moments when you are happy with people; but even the person that is annoying you at the moment, even the person who cut you off on the highway, even the person that is angering you. Everyone. We ARE ALL CONNECTED. Remember.

Catch yourself before the surface, ego self emerges and takes over. Remember your true essence. See that person in the moment as a Divine essence. Truly see their core essence. I find it helpful to say to myself "I acknowledge and honor you as a light being." I will also visualize a being of light within them. As I do this, I align myself with their true Divine self, as well as to Source. I am connected at the deeply true level. No matter what surface illusionary issue that is happening, I am aligned with true soul. I am soul to soul, divine to divine and heart to heart. The true meaning of Namaste is: "The divine in me, sees the divine in you. And when you are in that place in you and I am in that place in me, we are one." We are One. Remember.

We don't have to be around the people that are aggravating us or hurting us, in anyway, all the time. But for the time that we do need to be around them, we can choose to allow our inner being not to be affected by their antics. We can choose to continue to stay in our power, remember our divine selves and be in our Inner Peace. Yes, we will need to stand our ground at times, but we can do this from our Divine core self. We can do this and not allow our power to be taken, but rather to give something back that is divine. Seeing all beings as Divine assists you in remaining in your true self and emerging more of your true self in the process.

Remember our connection during every part of the day. Little things can trigger your brain to bring yourself back to that place. Your brain does not know when you are feeling something that is happening now or if you are just remembering a memory. In either case your will still receive the physical and emotional effects of whatever is happening, whether it is a memory or actually happening at that moment. So remember the inner peace you've felt before, remember the good moments in every moment you can and the more you do this every day, the more you will bring about this Inner Peace. The more inner peace will grow within you and the more you awaken to your true self at all times. For most of us it's a natural balanced progression, so if you keep doing this every day, you *will* see benefits throughout your entire life. You may even notice that things go more easily in life. You will not be adding to the negative spiral of ego thinking. You will just be aligned with the Divine.

Remember, the Universe supports you in all ways, always! I find it helpful to even recite this mantra as I am aligning with the universe with visualizing myself as a light being. "The Universe supports me in ALL WAYS, always. I am fully supported and aligned with the Universe. I am aligned with the Universe and my Divine destiny. I am Divine."

See the Divine in everyone you encounter. No matter who they are, no matter what story you associate with them, no matter the judgments you process about them, no matter the physical exterior of them, no matter who they mirror back to you. See the Divine in others. And see the divine in you.

Remember. Remember that divine essence in those that you come in contact with. Even in those you see on TV and tiny acquaintances that are mere moments in your day: the doctor you visit, your co-workers, your boss, your friends, your "enemies" aka teachers and in everyone.

At your core essence you are the Divine. You are magical and beautiful and divine light. You are all that you want to be and more. You are the creator of all things. You are Source and the Source is you. At the inner core of your soul and your entire being you are the Divine. Can you feel it?

Since I am a visual person, when I visualize, it assists my connection to the energy and to the Divine. It enhances my intention in a major way. Visualize this Divine essence that you are within yourself. Every day, start your day with this knowing of your Divine energy. See it, feel it and be it because you are it. See it beam from deep inside of you and radiate out in all directions. And for others, I will see a person and I will visualize a brilliant light shining from their core, their divine essence. I will forget the outer image and only connect to that. When I do this I am at One with the other and with the Divine in a much higher vibration. Only purity exists. Pure bliss is all I feel.

An Angel came to me in court last week with this very reminder. I could have had intentions and recited them and exhausted a "trying" effort for a positive result. Or simply Be. I chose to simply be and beam positive loving energy for the highest and best, good of all. I then consciously chose to see the divine essence in all I encountered. To the judge making his decision, only divine loving Source energy. To my ex-husband who was there in contempt for not paying child support, again, only divine loving Source energy. I would close my eyes serene at this experience and simply Be. I simply asked for a positive outcome for all our highest and best, good. I was surprised to hear the judge send him to jail. However, I reminded myself that it was for the highest and best, good of all. So this is what the Divine decided was necessary. So be it. It is all divine.

Remember the core Divine essence within yourself. Connect to it every day! Many times a day! Remember the core Divine essence within everyone. Pure bliss flows from this connection or rather remembrance. Namastè.

You will see the people around you change before your eyes. As if transformed. You've shifted and aligned with their higher being and that will bring it out in them (in time or immediately depending on their own growth). Whether it does show on the outside or not, it is still working. The seed has been planted. And whether it shows or not you need not worry about it. It is not them, it is you that is shifting. And since we are all connected, we are all shifting and transforming. As you stay in this place of awareness and divine stillness, you are the change you wish to see in the world.

Love

Our heart center is our connection to Mother Earth and Father Sky. It is our center. We are all coming back to our heart center, Anahata Chakra; to Love. Love is our true connection to the All. There have been recent scientific studies that show our physical heart is actually made up of an entire nervous system of its own, separate from the rest of the body's nervous system. Think about that. Our heart center is our connection to Source. As we work with our heart connection our evolution expands.

Remember the Universe is for you. The Universe and the world are connected to you and you to it. Love yourself unconditionally and you will see the world love you. Remember to send love to yourself many times a day or rather ALL the time. Life is blissful. You attract more love into your life because that is what you are seeing in you. And as you treat yourself with unconditional love, others will feel this and treat you the same way. You are the first person who should receive love when you wake up in the morning. When you rejuvenate yourself with this remembrance you can serve humanity in kind.

Something I try to do every day is to look at myself in the mirror and tell myself that I love me. I say "I acknowledge and honor you as a Light Being" and send unconditional love to myself. It is powerful to do this in the mirror. I feel this will truly assist you in not only liking yourself again but loving yourself. Try it. Do it for longer than a few days. Try it for 21 days or more! You will beam divine love. Others will notice something new in your eyes and in your being, even if they can't articulate it. Love is the key. Love is who you are at the core of your essence. Love, love, love.

Now take this one step further and honor the Divine Spark of Love in others. When you see another on the street, at work, in your home and at the grocery store really see them. Really smile. Really look into their eyes and connect with the Divine Spark within them. They may not know or understand. They may only feel your pure joy at the connection you've just made. But you know you've connected with them at the highest level. Send them love whether they feel it or not. Send Love from your heart to their heart. Intend that you connect with their highest soul. Feel the Divine within every living being. You can do this with people and things. I do this with Nature a lot. It is so easy to feel and spread this love while in stillness (our true way of being).

Come Back To Your Heart

You can access the inner realms through your heart. Your heart truly does hold all the answers and all-encompassing peace. Whenever I take even a tiny moment to remember and focus on my heart, peace floods my system. It's pretty amazing actually. My heart is my soul.

For instance, the Universe had been sending me messages recently to stop looking outside myself for answers. But I don't always take the hint unless it's a pretty blunt hint. So I scheduled myself a reading with a highly recommended trance channeler. And on three failed attempts I had to wake up and listen. The Universe stopped the first attempt at a reading due to a client's (of this reader) Husband being near death. The second time I was able to get through but the connection on the phone was static-y. So we rescheduled to give her time to talk to the phone company. I waited to see if the Universe would intervene a third time and it did. This wonderful reader had to go tend to another client and their passing or their loved ones passing (again). So that was two out of the three reasons that had to do with a client's death. Intriguing. So I canceled the reading because I made a deal with the Universe that it would take three times if I were to take action. They did as I asked and I canceled to honor that agreement. I took the message. I need not go outside myself for answers anymore.

Although I know that teachings and readings have been very beneficial in my past and will be for many others to receive guidance outside of yourself. This guidance is priceless. I will say it again that I honor all the teachings, books and learning's in my path that will continue for me throughout my life. We are, after all, in this together. Everyone that I come in contact with is my teacher. Isn't life amazing! These people help you see the truth within you. Not only that the guidance finally leads you back to yourself to find the truth. So don't ever stop learning from others but listen to yourself as much for your inner truth. My heart does hold all the answers, as well as peace. Peace can flood your system anytime you take the extra moment to focus on your heart.

Just look within. Think of your heart. Feel your heart center; your energetic heart, not your physical heart. As was taught to me, you may even see a pink glowing star there. This is the center of your heart. All the answers you could ever ask are here. Look within. The Divine within you resides here. As I tap into my heart I feel it in my third eye, my crown and my whole being. I truly feel connected, centered and at peace here no matter what circumstances are going on around me. Unconditional love pours through me as I remember my heart.

You can tap into the Divine Source energy here and heal the self as well as those around you. If you experience a painful situation, breathe, place your hand on your heart and look in your heart. This is powerful. Peace is all that is emulated from your center. And peace breathes out into your whole being when you do this. Breathe . . . . Release . . . Can you feel it?

Chapter 27

Multi-tasking it out. Simplicity is in.

"Love the moment, and the energy of that moment will spread beyond all boundaries." ~ Corita Kent

Multi-tasking it out. Simplicity is in. Simplicity is the way of the future, or rather present. We have been toggling too much all at once and that makes it hard to focus on living in our present moment and enjoying each task we are doing *as* we are doing it. Life is truly simple. Our ego minds would have us thinking that this process of life and of awakening is intricate. When really it is very simple and the closer you get to realization the more you realize this as truth.

Be present. As much as possible, come back to doing one activity at a time. Working on one activity at a time allows you to truly live in the present moment. You are better able to appreciate what you are doing and the time it takes to do that one task. Your focus is stronger and this energy that you put into your current activity is more heightened. More love can be offered.

So instead of eating while watching television, just enjoy the food in your mouth. Savor the flavor as you chew each morsel. If you've eaten while watching TV you'll know that you almost don't remember eating, and usually tend to overeat. Instead of tending to household chores while trying to spend time with the kids, just do one first. As much as you can and within reason on a daily basis, give your children your undivided attention. Even if you are doing nothing but sitting with them while they play or do their homework, your presence is felt tremendously. Just sit and observe or play along. You will feel freer than you thought possible just by being with your children. Epiphanies and lessons abound as we watch our kids live in the present moment all the time. We see them have fun and forget about the past in every moment. We see them live life to the fullest.

Instead of instant messaging or emailing while in the middle of a major project, do the project without interruption. Shut down the email or instant messaging system (and the phone) and give all of your beautiful energy to the project at hand. The project will go more smoothly, be even more efficient and innovative with continued focus and attention to it. New ideas more easily come to you as you work on the project in the present moment. If you are constantly interrupted it makes your brain hard to open up to creativity and flow. We are hard-wired to work on one project at time and give all of ourselves to it. As you do this you open up to divine messages, creative options and epiphanies that might not have had the room to flow in if you were splitting your focus

Instead of focusing on many hobbies or passions (that you just can't seem to figure out which one you want to do so you split your time) pick one and put all your attention to it. When you have many hobbies you want to try, unsure of which one is your highest passion, it's helpful to really sit down and figure out which one suits you best for that moment. You are splitting your energies into too many directions and therefore not really affording any of those hobbies or passions enough love and attention to truly know where you focus should be. Take time, even make a pro's and con's list, sit in quiet meditation and see which one pulls at you the most for that timeframe. It's possible you'll touch on them all but give yourself time to truly feel out each one individually. You'll also benefit by feeling more balanced in your life as a whole.

Your energy is split when you focus on too many things at once. A beautiful way to think of this is from Deepak Chopra, "We need to remember just one principle: Whatever we put our attention on grows stronger as a result of the energy it derives from our attention. Whatever we take away our attention from disintegrates. So rather than focusing on possible catastrophes, why don't we use this as an opportunity for personal growth and evolution?"

A great way to bring peace into your life is to also decorate your home as simply as you would like your life. This is a feng shui technique. It need not be filled to the brim with knick knacks and clutter that you never even see anymore when you enter your home. You can have those things that you treasure and get rid of the rest. When we moved into our new space we had one wall with no photos. My Husband asked me what we should put there. I said, "Absolutely nothing!" It looks beautiful just the way it is and the Buddha statue I have on a shelf nearby really stands out. I feel at peace walking into our home. The peace I desire to continue in my life surrounds my home as much as possible.

Our ego stuff us full of beliefs and information that truly does not matter and is not even true at the very core of it. It's much simpler than our ego lets us believe. As we awaken we shed more and more beliefs that really don't matter and don't exist in our lives anymore. The more you do this, the more you realize how simple life can be and how simple life always was. It's hard to see when we have all these ego and conditioned beliefs.

You'll find more peace and harmony with your life as you come back to a simpler way of living. What's the rush anyway? It will all get done when it is divinely timed and perfect. No matter what is happening, we only have right now. Take it one step at a time is enough. The love and energy we have is right now. Try not to divide it up in one moment as much as you possibly can, but truly focus that love and energy in each present moment. Divine synchronicities and grace will be seen as you allow yourself to live simple and present. The more we come to a simpler way of living and being the more we wake up to true inner peace.

Easily Driven to Distraction

I know that distractions are in my daily life constantly! We can be easily distracted from our goals and desires. When you have a desire you are working to manifest, watch those distractions. I know this has been a huge challenge for me. The Angels have been bringing this up with me more and more this week than ever!

It's so easy to be distracted. The electronic distractions are unbelievable. From TV, Home Phone, Cell Phone, Ipod's, pagers, to Computers with Instant Messengers and Email! It's any wonder we get anything tangible accomplished. These gadgets are to make our life easier and enrich our lives, not rip us away from authentic connections and human contact.

Over time I have come to realize that not only are these time-wasting distraction they can be detrimental to our overall health in every way. Television, Radio, the negative news, drama shows, subliminal commercials, and negative music and so on can be extremely negative and fear-based. Remove yourself from such negative actions. I no longer watch, listen or read the news. I change the station when I hear negative songs or negative words in songs. I do my best to no longer watch shows that are negative, fear-filled or full of drama and victim play. I don't want anything negative to get into my subconscious. The more I removed myself from these experiences the more peaceful I felt. No more negative feedback here! Removing these negative distractions is a detox of the mind, body and soul. Embrace more positive elements into your life. Transcend the old ways.

We also need to focus. Distractions can build up and take away our focus from our true intentions. I want all of us to remember that yes, we must let go of what we desire once we have made the request, put forth the right amount of energy and have given gratitude. But we must know that putting forth the right amount of energy takes more than just a quick thought. If you think of a desire and then move on quickly to the next thought or distraction (from the phone, television, to a new thought or idea) you may not have given this enough focus and attention it requires to manifest. Ask your Angels for help in focusing.

Remember what Abraham-Hicks has said time and again: 17 seconds is all it takes! Focus with all your energy (visualize, think and feel the positive desire you choose) as if it's happening right now in this very moment. It actually IS happening in this very moment and then your magic takes hold for the Universe to manifest. If you can bring your focus up to 68 seconds you've quadrupled your power. These 68 seconds are equivalent to working 2,000 man hours! I'd say 68 seconds are definitely worth whatever your desire is.

Move away from Electronic distractions. Commune with nature. When in nature you can more easily hear your soul's call. No longer ignoring through distraction. And you can hear the Angels more clearly. Everything falls away. Look up. A beautiful blue sky, stars and moon. An Ocean. A forest. Your life is waiting. Your soul is calling. Step outside and breathe. Nature fills our soul and energies our body. It calls to us. It stills the mind as we can just allow ourselves to breathe and be. A quote by Lao Tzu says it best, "Nature does not hurry, yet everything is accomplished".

When you feel overly distracted and nothing seems to be working the way you desire, take a moment. Go outside; get in touch with nature again. Breathe in fresh air. Ground yourself to the Earth and let go of those worries. Leave the cell phone and IPod at home this time. Listen to your intuition and feel your desire, one desire at a time. Focus on only one. And really feel it with all of your being. If you can't get outside, just get to a place where you are free of distraction and can take a few minutes for yourself for this practice. You will rejuvenate on all levels as you give yourself time to breathe and focus. As you do this your desires manifest that much more quickly, that much more smoothly and that much more powerfully.

Distractions happen to me often. Just when I think I've set my intention for a desire, I've gone through it too quickly in order to get to the next thing on my list. I am constantly being reminded to take my time. There is no rush; especially when it comes to what we truly desire. But remember time and space is of no essence. They do not really exist. We can slow time and speed it up. We can be with someone who is on the other side of the world in mere moments if we choose. So relax, breathe and focus one intention at time. The Angels can more easily assist us as we take the time to be clear, listen and focus on our desires one beautiful feeling at a time.

"Whether we avoid something because it scares us or bores us, or because we think it will force a change we're not ready for, putting it off only creates obstacles for us. On the other hand, facing the task at hand, no matter how onerous, creates flow in our lives and allows us to grow." ~ Madisyn Taylor, Daily OM

Occasionally we avoid quiet moments because we don't want to hear the uncomfortable messages that are screaming at us to be heard. Sometimes it takes a few moments of listening and breathing through the issues to get to the other side and feel the peace that comes from simply allowing it to be there. Ignoring the uncomfortable thoughts will only compound on them and you'll eventually blow a gasket. So instead, listen to those thoughts. Hear the messages. Transmute the negative into positives and simply stay in the present moment. There is freedom here in the Now. A weight is lifted.

It's quite possible that you are distracted from really working on a specific desire because you are scared of it never coming, so in that sense you have already manifested it *not* coming. Maybe you are scared it *will* come so you don't take the time to really help it along to fruition. But in the end your desire is your desire. Fear is nothing till you give it power. If you give it power it will create the fearful event you don't want. Take the ego and fear out of the equation. Listen only to what makes you happiest and your higher self and Angels. All positive information flows more easily to you when you are in a neutral state of mind. Have a wish, but allowing it to either be there or not. It either is or it is not. It will either happen or it will not. It matters not, as long as you are always in your joy and happiness. Sharing love and bliss with those around you in whatever way you desire is all there is.

Chapter 28

Create a Sacred Space

Create a sacred space in your home that is just for you. No one else is aloud in this space. A room that you have to yourself is ideal. If you don't have that much space, then place it in one corner of a room for yourself. Maybe in your bedroom.

Make this space fit who you are. Put up a photo or two that emulate you and one of nature. If this space is by a window that outlooks nature—even better. You may desire to set up an altar with crystals and a statue of something desirable to you. I have a Buddha with flowers and a Bali-Tibetan Bell. Having something on your altar that brings in the four elements (Earth, Air, Fire and Water) is a beautiful way to bring nature to you. Set up some cozy pillows for comfort and allow yourself to sink into your being state. This space is just for you. You can go to this space to meditate or to be with yourself in times of rejuvenation.

By having this sacred space you allow yourself the room to breathe and just be. Every time you go back to this space you bring more peaceful energy to this space and it is in turn infused with more of this peaceful intention. You'll start to notice that just by entering this space you almost immediately feel more peaceful.

> "Enveloping ourselves in a peaceful environment helps us cultivate peace within. Since our lives are filled with so much stimulation and distractions, it is often difficult to maintain a feeling of inner calm. Creating a space that is immersed in stillness, however, allows us to bring our focus within and without the diversions of the world around us. This alignment between outer and inner world gives us a sense of comfort and quietude that makes it easier to recognize that our true nature is in fact one of gentle calm. Being in a place that soothes your soul and quiets your mind will let you find a deeper and more resonant part of yourself that is peace today." ~ Madisyn Taylor, Daily Om

I mentioned Feng Shui briefly in Chapter 4 as a method regarding Clutter Clearing. Feng Shui can also be brought in here for your sacred space. You may want to research Feng Shui further to see what portion of your home resonates with the Bagua for a spiritual place of solitude. Remember that at its very core even Feng Shui is intention-based. So go with what feels good above ALL else!

Next, I'd like to give you tips on keep your sacred space clean and clear for the strongest most peaceful connections when you come to your space. This goes beyond the obvious physical cleaning of your space. However, a good sweeping will bring in beautiful new energies and spruce up your space fast when you need a quick fix.

Smudging

Smudging (burning Sage) is an ancient Native American practice that removes negative stagnant energy from your space.

Clearing your home on a regular basis (at least monthly) is good protocol, just as cleaning your house physically is. You want your home clean of icky stagnant energy, so as to not attract anything of that same vibration. Sage will get rid of all negativity in your house. Go room to room. It's the smoke from the sage that gets rid of the negativity. So if you feel the need to do it in more than just one spot in the room, like every corner, etc., then by all means do so! This is a good method to get rid of negativity and a lot of the times negative entities. You should do this on a periodic basis. Once is never enough. Because of strong negative emotions from fights, etc., and if new negative ghosts arrive, this will aid in getting rid of those negativities. They say that White Sage is the best. Either kind you find will work though.

When you feel the need to cleanse your home of negativities (emotions lingering from past arguments and/or upset, etc.), smudging is the most common and most highly recommended process. There are many reasons to smudge and I can't think of one not to smudge. There is no adverse affects. Simply said Sage rids your house of negativity. So get yourself some Sage. White Sage is said to be the best, but any Sage is effective. If you can't use Sage for whatever reason (maybe it's the smell or your neighbors, etc.) try getting Sandalwood incense. This is a close second to Sage. I also prefer to use Nag Champa when I can't use sage. A third option to Sage or incense is to use a spray that has been blessed by you or another that includes essences or herbs of your choosing that pack a good protection and cleansing punch.

You can Sage yourself, your home, your car, any object for that matter and so much more. Some say they Sage their home as regularly as they do their weekly or bi-weekly cleaning of their home. And others say monthly is a good practice. Do what feels right for you. When Saging your home be sure to focus strongly on Door Frames: Front and Back door! Go through EACH room, and focus strongly in every corner and windows. If you can (if you own the place), try to also smudge outside the home, on the grounds and by windows and doors. Be sure to leave a window open in each room so the energy has a place to exit. When you start, say the following excerpt 3 times. Also say the following saying again 3 times at each Door you have in your home:

"I call on the spirits of the North, South, East and West. Please come forth. Banish any and all negativity surrounding (((Me, my son, my job, my house, etc.—this is in parenthesis because this is where you will use your own words of what you would like cleansed of all negativity))). I know not who, I know not their name, please send it back from whence it came. Thank you!" Three TIMES.

Chapter 29

Hear Your Soul's Call

Hear Your Soul's Call—Follow Your Passion

As you follow your bliss you connect more with your Divine self. You are meant to do what makes YOU happy. You are meant to follow your joy, your passion, whatever drives you in your happiness. This is what you will emulate out into the world. The Divine is you and you are the Divine. As you follow your true calling in life you are experiencing your unique self. And as you do this the Divine is always experiencing itself as you. Dance your dance. Each of us has a unique ability (or gift) that is what we are meant to do in life. For some it's clothing design, others it's farming the land for food and others still have a calling for entertainment in dancing or acting, etc. Each gift is ours to share with the community and the world. Do not be afraid to show who you truly are in all ways. As you allow yourself to be who you truly are you surrender to bliss and self. You align with the Divine.

It is said that in the new world in the days to come we will each live and offer our unique gifts in the community and there will be no money exchange. Each person's offering is in exchange for another person's offering. So we are all taken care of within the community and there is a sense of sharing and love. Some cultures around the world already follow this way of living. By some, they are seen as poverty stricken, but really they are living in peace and bliss. They are happy offering their gift to the community and enjoying life. In time we will all get there. Follow your bliss; it's your Spiritual Compass.

How do we tune in to our Spiritual Compass? We all have a guidance system from within. It's our intuition. As we awaken and ascend our intuition becomes more open and easily attainable. You know that pull you get when you really feel you should go a certain direction or take a certain path. That's our guidance system. Some like to call it gut instincts.

Take steps to hear your intuition or your soul's call everyday. For example, take a time to get quiet with yourself. You can meditate if you choose to, or simply take away all distractions to really hear the messages from within. When you turn off the TV, radio, ipod, computer and phone, as well as remove yourself from an active environment, you hear what's really screaming at you from within.

Hear your soul's call. Your soul is calling but many are misinterpreting it and many others are running to various distractions. Such as: to the refrigerator to fill up your belly, or to the television, or the store to buy one more thing, or having meaningless conversation/gossip. Basically any distraction your ego can think up. But you're not hungry. You don't need that extra item from the store. Will you remember that show you watched on TV tomorrow? Talking about others is a mirror on yourself. All of these distractions are taking you away from what you truly desire most, what you are really hungry for. Your Soul is hungry for Love, Compassion, Acceptance and Purpose.

Follow your Soul's call. Stop before your next distraction. Take three deep breaths. Then ask yourself, are you really hungry? Ask yourself do you really need that item you were about to go buy? Do you really want to hear or talk nasty about your soul siblings? (Who are just growing with their own fears and doubts, wants and desires, just as you, only in their own way.) Do you really want to distract yourself from your Soul's Calling. It's calling to you now. When the answer to these questions are honestly and truthfully answered by your inner self, you can then ask a new question. What does my Soul desire? Immediately thoughts, feelings and happy ideas will FLOW to you! LISTEN! Hear the call.

Passion, Joy and Love are common feelings for you to feel in EVERY moment now. And these are the feelings that will come up when you hear your Souls' desires. What feels exciting truly is your next step. If there are many things, choose the most exciting. The one that feels the most passion, joy and love! That is your next adventure. There is no need to go back to the old ego ways of stifling down your soul's call with distractions. Now you can tell your ego enough is enough and hear your inner Souls' truth.

Live in the mystery and magic of creation. Feel the magic of all your of your power. You are part of the all-knowing and all-loving power. There is so much more to you than you know. Truly start to connect with the aliveness within you. See the unlimited potential and unlimited possibilities you have to share with the Self and with the world. You truly CAN do anything! You are powerful and transcendent. Show it off! Follow your heart and enjoy hearing your souls' call in every moment!

Divinely Inspired Action

Taking divinely inspired action is the next logical necessary step once you've heard your soul's call. We are living on this planet in this dimension for many reasons. One is to really live and enjoy life. We all receive divine guidance from within; from our hearts, from our Higher Selves, from our

Angels. Sometimes it is a bang on our heads and many times it's very soft and gentle. When you receive inspired action to do something, don't hesitate. Go. Do it! Inspired action is *not* something you feel you should do for someone else. It is not something you do if you feel pressured. This is not inspired action. Inspired action feels very divine and very true to your nature. You will know when you receive this action as it speaks to your very core. And it feels familiar at times and like you can do nothing but whatever this action speaks to. At other times, a lot of the times, it feels subtle because it's so familiar. It is a small still voice within you saying, "You should do this. You should try this. See what happens." It's not always going to be a huge, strong, in-your-face message to take action. It will be small at first and then may get larger if you choose to ignore the tiny messages coming to you.

This is the same with manifesting. You will do the fun positive thoughts and energy flowing steps but you must follow through. You must take action. You can't simply sit there and expect it to come to you without you actually doing something when the divine action comes to you of what you should do. For example, your dream is to be a doctor. You manifest by visualizing yourself as a doctor, you think positive. But if you don't fill out the college applications and actually go to the school that resonates then you may never get to be the doctor you visualized. There are action steps that will come to you to naturally take for the results to occur.

Remember: follow your bliss; it's your spiritual compass. Imagine the blissful feeling you feel when you are following inspired action! It feels amazing. Whatever you are drawn to, go do it! If it feels good within then that is your bliss. Your heart guides you to the right path always. This inner pull is divine guidance for a job, for a creative task, for an experience you are meant to have, for a person you are meant to meet by following this guidance. The Divine knows more than we do. There is a mask over our eyes of the future blueprint. But the Divine knows more. So the Divine Source will send you inner pulls, blissful feelings and synchronistic events that guide you on your path. It is always there pulling you along. It is our ever constant assurance. This is true freedom and peace, as all you need to do is live in every moment following what pulls at your bliss!

Every time you take inspired action you are saying YES to the Universe. You are saying, 'Yes give me more of this!' And by the Laws of Attraction you receive more! And a positive spiraling affect and beautiful experiences flow into your life, as if by magic. All because you listened and took action. By taking action you also give others permission to do the same. You give permission to your kids, your siblings, your parents, your friends, your co-workers, and people you don't know to take action themselves! Likewise, when you don't, you also send that frequency out into the world and that flows back to you as well. It's your choice whether you take action or not. But observe. See how it feels when you don't. See the not-so-wonderful experiences that occur when you don't. Then take action from divine inspired action and see the amazing synchronicities and miracles that flood your life when you do! Taking inspired action is powerful.

Live Your Destiny of Service

Each of us are at different stages in our awakening process. As we awaken we will be guided to find out or rather may question what it is we are to do here on this planet as a way to contribute. Our destiny of service. Each of us has a divine role to express. Shine forth your true self. It's time. We each have an inner purpose and an outer purpose. Your inner purpose is always to remember and awaken the Divine being that you already are. This section is dedicated to your outer purpose. Your outer purpose is what you decide you will Be in this life in any given moment while holding on to your inner purpose as primary. You'll have questions as to what truly is your unique offering. Truly following your bliss is your spiritual compass. I've laid out some steps that surround learning your destiny of service. Many follow the inner guidance within them and are doing their divine service now. And for those that have questions or would like further guidance as to what that may be for them in this moment, this section is for you. Following are steps to living your destiny of service:

Step 1. Find Your Truest Passion—Your Bliss
Step 2. Cultivating Your craft
Step 3. Taking Divine Action

Step 1: Find Your Truest Passion—Your Bliss

Your Divine destiny is also known as your passion. Whatever your passion is in life is also what you are meant to do in life as your self-expression to service the Divine. Whatever brings you joy and happiness, whatever feels good to you, IS your Destiny. There is something that is innate and organic within each of us. It is that which drives us to bring fulfillment and uplifting experiences to us. It is our Divine destiny to find and follow our truest passion. Because our truest passion is also our expression of Divinity. And that is our bliss. Whatever brings you joy, peace and bliss is your driving force and expression in life. As I like to say follow your bliss, it's your spiritual compass. If you don't already know what it is you'd like to do in life there are some great questions you can ask yourself:

- What do I like to do?
- What is the driving goal of my life?
- What would I do even if I wasn't getting paid to do it?
- When I think of a time when I totally got lost in what I was doing, what was I doing?
- Does this job idea(s) feel right?

I've found many more questions for you to ask yourself like this and many valuable exercises that I find truly helpful in Karen Bishop's book, *Remembering your Soul's Purpose*. You may find this book quite helpful.

We all have a talent or gift we are called to do. This is your divine service that feels good to your Soul and anyone else who benefits is a definite perk. It might not be something you do full time but only part-time. We are each unique in how and what we will offer. Whatever it may be, it is worth pursuing. The more we follow our true passions and are in a state of allowing, the more those wonderful doors will open.

What excites you? You'll know because you'll feel it inside. When you have something in mind that you like doing or would like to do, you feel happy, free and excited! This is your higher self sending you and your body a signal to say that you are right on track. This is it! Follow this path and you *will* be 100% fully supported.

How do you know if you are close to your divine calling? If you are feeling stressed, worried, anxious or fearful, you are not in your divine self. If you feel good, happy, enthusiastic about where you are and what you are doing or not doing, then you are in the right place!!! It's that simple. Your feelings ARE your spiritual divine compass. Always check in with yourself and ask yourself how you feel within. Truly listen to your heart.

You may say that what you are truly passionate about seems far-fetched. What part of you is making you feel this way? Is there an embedded, even subconscious, belief that may have even come from childhood? These are some great questions to become more aware of and ask yourself. What part of you must believe that this is farfetched? Is it possibly a way to hold you back through a fear from your ego? Here is where we need to decipher between your Divine guidance and your Ego. Your ego has a purpose and that's usually to protect you. However, it gets off the wall a LOT! If you hear a thought and it doesn't feel good to you, more than likely it's your ego trying to instill a base fear in you to keep you from expanding i.e., for fear that you won't succeed, fear that you won't be supported, fear that you even will succeed, etc. Again, fear equals "False Evidence Appearing Real".

In the hypnosis training I received we were taught techniques in getting the participant to their core belief. (Core beliefs are also discussed in more depth in Book Two *Divine Embrace*). We all have core beliefs that we received either in past lives or in this life, say as a child. You can look back at your childhood, your parents and wonder about their dynamic and see how that ties in to you thinking that your passion is farfetched or beyond your reach. There may be some insights that come to you. When you have a base fear, just ask yourself what part of you makes you have this fear. Then when you have that answer, ask again, what part of you believes this and why. Take the *first* answer that comes each time and eventually you'll find something that rings true from within. Then work on transmuting that core belief. Just start to become aware that if it isn't something on the surface that is easy to crush like a bug, it could be a more embedded belief that you will pull from the archives of your brain and re-program yourself to think and feel positive about your new ventures.

Something to remember: Just by wondering and asking about your passion, you are manifesting it. And just by becoming more awake and aware of any fears that hinder the growth into those passions, you shine a light on them and start to transmute them into pure light. In essence, you squash them like a bug. Your core belief will decide what you bring into your life. The Universe sends us exactly what we request. So what you see is what you are asking for, what your vibration matches. The good and the not-so-good. Change your core belief into a positive and believe you deserve all you desire. Then you start to emanate that frequency and receive more positive results.

Remember: "Your strongest fear is your strongest belief!" (Bashar). So change your fear (your core belief) and become a new higher vibration and attract more of positive higher vibrational experiences. I am repeating myself, but only because it's true and the more we hear something the more it embeds itself into our brains for our subconscious to listen.

And when one door closes another opens. Even if you believed you were heading in the right direction, remember that a new door will be provided. Maybe even a new path that you are more aligned with. And most important of all, when that door closes you must then trust that another door truly will open. And then . . . it will. You are always supported. The Universe supports you in all ways, always.

Remember that we can still be in our bliss even while we are *on the way to our passion of service*. It's the journey that is to be enjoyed always. Striving for something better without having attachments to the outcomes is a challenge for some. What is living in "The Way" is to simply serve in however you are intuitively guided to serve with joy in every step, withOUT attachments to the results. When you have an attachment to the result, you are bringing your ego into it and producing more unnecessary karma. Simply allow yourself to emerge naturally. Simply do your service, whatever that is, wherever you are in the process, with joy and happiness in the moment, in every moment. And as you ride the natural waves of life, intuitive Divine guidance flows to you and you move in joy always.

Law of Attraction and allowing

When you've decided you know what it is you'd like to pursue as your passion, you must start putting it out there. The Universe answers EVERYTHING we think and FEEL about. There is no question that we are 100% responsible for all things that come to us. So the jobs you've gotten thus far are everything that has been inside of you already and are there as stepping stone points for your own purposes. Each job has taught you many things about yourself thus far. So start to FEEL good about your passion. What you are doing is simply aligning with your divine calling. Your vibrations are a match as it is your purpose. As Wayne Dyer said in his fantastic movie *Ambition to Meaning*, you are not attracting something to you, but simply aligning with what is already yours. Start to visualize yourself doing your passion. Feel how fantastic you will—ARE feeling living your passion NOW. Remember, as your vibrations matches what you desire, it automatically comes to you by Law of Attraction. So as you feel what you desire, this is you resonating with your passion and drawing it to you. Your feeling is your vibration. As you match your frequency aka how you feel to your desire, you will receive it as you are matching the like frequency of that desire. As you FEEL it as if it is RIGHT NOW, then it truly happens RIGHT NOW.

There is a 17 second gauge of feeling to practice. Feel and visualize this for 17 seconds. All you need to do is 17 seconds of feeling something without an opposite feeling whatsoever and you've then manifested it!!! And if you can do it for that long, do it for another 17 seconds and another. If you get up to 68 seconds, you have done what's equal to 2000 "normal" 3D waking life working hours!!! That's a FULL year's work in a straight 68 seconds. This is explained in much more depth in an article by Abraham at Abraham-Hicks.com. AWESOME! Try it. Again, all you need to do is 17 seconds of feeling something without an opposite feeling whatsoever and you've then manifested it!!! Remember that even after your 17 seconds are up, NOT to feel the opposite or you bring THAT to you instead. If you notice negative feelings come up, CHANGE them. Think positive and BE the new passion you desire.

Another thing is that you can draw what you desire. Draw it and use it as a Vision/Dream board. This can be a drawing or cut-outs from a magazine. The visuals will be the job you desire. So, for example, if it is becoming a yoga teacher, you may place a picture of a woman teaching yoga poses to students. You get the idea. Whatever way draws in the energy to you the most is the best way for you to do it. We are all unique and must do it the way we resonate with. There are seven different ways to learn something and it's helpful to have a balance of all of them to integrate the result. Some of us are visual, some tactile, some a little of both, etc. Again, as they say, thought, word, deed and action are potent when utilized simultaneously. Stimulate your senses. Put this on a board and hang it up in your office or place where you will see it often. Every time you see this visual think happy thoughts about it and FEEL it as if you are living it. You are a manifesting machine! ☺

How you feel about yourself matches what you will attract to you in life. How you see yourself from deep inside is how others will see you and is exactly what you will manifest in the present and future moments. And what you do for yourself is exactly what you will receive from others. So when you start to expect more from another that you don't even give to yourself, then you will be disappointed. Don't give your power away to that frame of being. Give to yourself as if giving to a child you love. Give the same to others. And watch magic happen in your life. See yourself as a magical being and see others the same. Watch the magical realm of life open up before your eyes just by opening up and surrendering to this new vantage point. The advantage is that when you see more beauty, expect more beauty, and give more beauty, you receive more beauty.

For example, I was extremely overweight. At 225 pounds I had given up. I surrendered to my state as a "chubby" person. It was then that I realized what I had done in my earlier years. When I was at a respectable weight for my body, I felt fat. I saw myself as a fat person and over the course of that thinking and ultimately that way of being, I did grow into the vision I saw myself as. I became overweight because I felt overweight. Low self-esteem was a contributing factor to my inner belief as well. Even though I was not overweight at the time, I manifested it into being, simply because on the inside that is how I saw myself. So when I looked into the mirror and realized what I had done, I woke up. I realized I needed to now see myself healthy and thin. I needed to gain that same perception of myself on the inside but as a healthy and thin person.

Over the course of some other life enhancing changes and emotional transformations, I started to really feel myself as a thin person. As I did this I also made smarter choices. I started a beautiful workout routine with Denise Austin (who exposed me to yoga as well) and started eating much less and much healthier than I had in years. The key is the combination of the *healing visualizations, law of attraction* and *never eating unconsciously or emotionally.* In eleven months I shed 90 pounds and I felt great! At 29 years old I felt better than I had in high school when I was thin. A transformation occurred within me with a simple intention of viewing myself healthy and thin from within. You can take this example and use it to work for you in living in the state of being you desire.

Now start asking yourself: What Does the perfect divine job feel like? Continue asking yourself that question and get yourself to the feeling of it and you're there. Stay there and if you lose that feeling, keep asking. What does it feel like to do (such and such) _____? Feel it, see it, live it, BE it. Enjoy!

One avenue for you to do what you love now is if there is a way that you can volunteer yourself in some fashion (at least to begin with); this will align you with those energies. You will start to match your vibration to what drives you and your excitement. Your passion. You will attract more of those situations to you the more you expose yourself to what you would like to do. The more you do this, the more you will believe it's possible for you to do that. Then you will attract people and experiences that tell you just that and you will be presented by the Universe with ways you can pursue your passion for the long-term. It's amazing how energy works!

Now, each of us is unique in our process to our passions. Some of us may have a couple of core things we'd like to do on a consistent basis and some of us have just one. We each will do it in our own time. Some will take on their passion part-time and keep a full time job. Some will start part-time and then go full time thereafter. No way is wrong. All are right. Some make a huge leap into their passion and take off. Some take the route of a slow progression. It's all in how you feel is best for you. There are stepping stones you can take that will get you there in a wonderful divinely timed way. Maybe there is schooling needed for certain talents or gifts that is required before starting or required while you follow that passion. (More on this under step 2 to follow.) Either way, as long as you are doing even one thing towards your goal daily you will start to feel more and more fulfilled deep in your soul. You are always 100% supported. So I say go for it!

"It usually takes about 30 days to change a habit. Not because you need 30 days. You could do it in 68 seconds if you could hold your vibration there, but you have to consciously make that decision. . . . .

The Universe does not know whether the vibration that you're offering is because of something you're observing or something you're remembering or something that you are imagining. It just receives the vibration and answers it with things that match it. And every part of the Universe including the cells of your body begin to respond to that vibration."
~ Abraham-Hicks.com

Step 2: Cultivating Your Craft

We are now highlighting the cultivating stage. When you've come to the stage of having awakened and you know what it is you desire doing as your passion, your joy, your hat for society, there is usually a step where you will cultivate that passion. Whatever requires developing will take place within this step. If you know what you'd like to do but feel more schooling is in store for you to master this skill—then go for it. You may feel a lot of practice is involved to fine tune this wonderful talent of yours. It is all you, so your essence will go into whatever it is you are doing. Someone doing the same thing will have a different essence to the skill. We are each unique and even in doing the same thing there are unique differences. Add your special touch to whatever it is you are cultivating as your craft or Divine Destiny of Service.

This step is perfect for you to really see what it is you want to do. It really helps you get to the nitty gritty of your passion and the actual steps you will take. Rather than wasting time in areas you wouldn't need to or that would really make life more challenging or difficult. (Note here that having a difficult time is not part of our path in Ascension, the end result is about enjoying our passions.) This time helps you to really embrace your truest passion and not allow things that are NOT in-line with your truest passion to "accidentally" sneak in there anymore. This is why the cultivating step is sometimes a necessary step. Here you are sure to mold yourself and your truest passions together. Really feel your inner yearnings and again continue to ask yourself the questions from *Step 1: Find Your Truest Passion—Your Bliss*, when you are unclear.

This step takes much patience and sometimes tolerance of doing something that isn't quite in-line with your passion just yet. For instance, my Husband, Don, is very into drumming and creating music. It's his bliss. He is in a few bands, one of which is a rock band for kids called *Character Rising* (found at www.characterrising.com if you are intrigued). Don and the band continue to cultivate their practice by working together, creating new songs, practicing over and over and building a fan-base by marketing their band and playing at shows (sometimes for free). While doing the cultivating stage Don is also a financial advisor full time in order to have the means to pursue his truest passion. Once the music takes off at a better rate he may be able to cut back on the other business. He will play it out and see how the chips fall while he stays in his passion as often as possible. Don is able to continue to cultivate his craft by modifying his full time business to something that better caters to his passion in music. He is still making ends meat and thriving in his passion.

So in this stage your juices are flowing. Your seeds are sprouting and you are taking daily action towards your truest passion. This is a time for building your energies.

In this process you might ask yourself if you are insane. Things like: "What makes me think I can do something that I like doing and make a decent living? I should be doing a "real" job!? I don't deserve to take it easy. I have to work hard to make money. What would people say? I don't think I can do this? It's a pipe dream and I have to get back to "reality", etcetera, etcetera."

These questions are your ego working overtime! These questions come from years and lives of conditioning you've been put through as well as limiting beliefs from this life and past lives. As Julie Meggles-Brenner from Kajama.com states, "We're at a tricky point where we identify more and more with our higher selves, yet we're not totally free of the lower vibrations that could make us vulnerable to undesirable experiences. For example, we may be full of faith and trust, but if there is karma to be resolved with someone or some buried wound, fear or issue at work in our subconscious mind, we can still attract the sort of experience."

It's time to un-condition those thoughts and create better thoughts. As you create better thoughts, you create better emotions that create better energy patterns. The more you do this, the more THIS becomes a habit and you attract only positive results of being in your passion. You can and do deserve to be happy NOW, not later.

In this cultivating stage you are able to really take the time to get clear about what you desire. As the path becomes clearer it is easier to manifest wonderful results. This cultivating stage is congruent to the progress you have made and are about to make. You are in-line with your desires and this is the Universe's way of giving you the perfect opportunity to craft your passion for living. This is a way to really sink your teeth into what you desire by reading about it, taking in any more knowledge that may assist you with your craft, setting the stage for when you will start this craft in a more full-time capacity.

Part of the cultivating stage is manifesting from within. Truly think about and visualize you doing your craft. See it, feel it and be it. As you do this more experiences and opportunities will come to you that may be big steps or are seemingly small but worth doing. Take the small and big hints from the Universe and your Angels. You can always ask God or the Angels to help you with clarity as they love to shine the light stronger for you where they can for your highest and best, good.

Where something may not seem clear and may even seem cloudy, even after you ask for guidance, step back. Take a breather and live in some of the joyful moments in your life. As you become more neutral you are able to see more clearer what steps need to happen. Remember, it is not about pushing or forcing yourself; as this will only make this harder on yourself. It is about going with the flow of what will be and what already is. Just be in every present moment and you will see what matters now is only Now.

For those already in step 3 and taking action, you are there. You've already spent the time and energy into finding your passion and have really worked wonders in just being in your happy blissful state as often as possible no matter what you are doing. One thing you will notice in the taking action stage is that you will still transform your passions and even change them completely. You continuously evolve, fine-tune and transform as you ascend. So you may be coming back to the *Cultivating Your Craft Step* a number of times for a new passion or fine-tuning a current one as it evolves. The core essence is that you are always staying true to your wants and desires; your joy. You will each be at different levels and that is okay. It is not possible to be at the same level as everyone else. We each evolve in our own way, in our own time. This all integrates together in a beautiful process.

Sometimes the funnest part of the cultivating stage is doing nothing! There are times when you will just have nothing to do and all you can see for some time is peace and living in whatever situation you are in now. This need not be a boring or worry-filled stage. Enjoy relaxation, because soon you'll be entrenched deep in your passion. These moments of bliss are perfect for you to build, create and just be with your desires. There is balance in rest and action. This is a time for both. Dream your dream as you move through the Cultivating step. Know you are always on the right path and everything is always in Divine order.

Step 3: Taking Divine Action

Okay, it's time! You're awakened. You know what your service or passion in life is! You've taken the time to cultivate your craft. Now, it's time you go out there and DO IT! It's not enough to figure out what you'd like to do in life. It's not enough to percolate those passions and cultivate that craft. You must then take that leap of faith and be in your bliss. Take divine action. For some, you're beyond the first two steps and are already here in the *Take Divine Action* mode. This is the last piece I have written with good reason. I've cultivated till I was blue in the face and had to face facts that I'm there. It's time. My time to show the Universe that I am taking what gifts, learning's, and abilities they've given me and am willing to take action and show the world in whatever fashion is right for ME.

Taking action on showing who you truly are to the world and most importantly to yourself is the path to bliss. As you are true to yourself, to who you are and taking those steps to always remain in that state of true divine nature within yourself, you become the divine being you decided you would be while living this Earthly life. You'll feel bliss in all moments, even the uncomfortable ones; but none-the-less bliss. As you realize you are always a Divine Being of light! And expressing that light within you is your divine right, your divine power and your divine calling. Whatever that is for you is truly your bliss.

So what do you do when taking action? This can be the easy part, as long as you've done your homework. You simply put yourself out there. You've taken the required schooling, learnings, and practiced your skill and know you are ready. So now, as you follow your intuition on just where you should go, you will put your offerings out there to the world. This may be looking for that right job in that right place and posting your resume, taking the interviews that are offered and accepting the job offer that feels like the best fit for you.

Or this may be you putting your own business out there to the world. So when in the *Cultivating Your Craft* stage you would have already come up with marketing ideas and creations to let people know you're in business. So now you can put these ideas out there to the world. This may require some capital to begin with but with the right research you are well-prepared and working your way towards following these action steps. You will be guided on what space is right for your type of business and will check out possibilities with a realtor or by yourself and move into the right space for you. Then comes the fun creating-your-space part. It's your business so create the look and feel that fits, not only your business but, YOU! It's YOU that is drawing in the clients, so it is you they want to see. Check in with your budget and see what you can do as your business grows. As it grows you will be able to do more of the things you like to make the space feel more aligned with you.

In this stage of the game you would have already began noticing that things were falling into place before you even began to think about taking action. Just by your prior steps of deciding upon a passion that fits you and cultivating your craft, you've built up the energy and the Universe is already providing you with things, people and situations that will assist you in getting there synchronistically! This is a wonderful sign that you've been on the right track! Take these serendipitous events and allow them to work their magic for you. It doesn't have to always be hard or challenging. Sometimes it's rather simple and easy to fall into your rightful place! You've probably noticed these signs in ALL of these stages. That is how energy works. Enjoy working in a new reality! It's not really work when it's FUN!

You will notice that as you get into the *Taking Divine Action* step that there are some "starts" and "stops". These are meant to happen to guide you in the right direction if you have veered off track or to simply allow a little more time to go by so that things happen in the right Divine timing. These "starts" and "stops" are stepping stones to ready you for getting out there full speed ahead, full throttle, no turning back. These are seemingly part of the *Cultivating Your Craft* stage, as you need these starts and stops in order to better prepare. To know what's out there for you and how you should go about different situations as they arise. You'll also notice as you reach this stage that there may be a few moments that I like to call "Breath of fresh air" time. Where you are there, you know what you are to do, but the "take action" time isn't quite there yet. Timing is everything. Sometimes you have to wait a bit for people to catch up to you in order to go full throttle on your strategy for taking action. And that is perfect. You get to breathe, rejuvenate and relax. We all need that balance in our life.

Here are some law of attraction affirmations you can choose to keep you on track. These can assist you in knowing what your passion is, following that passion, cultivating that passion, keeping up with the evolving of this passion (through new learning's, networking, etc.). Please do modify these to fit you. There are many varieties of affirmations out there. So take these as a small example of what you can do. Repeat this many times a day. Believe them and believe in yourself:

- I give myself permission to be fulfilled and follow my passion.
- Clarity and focus comes easily to me.
- I exceed my expectations and am recognized for my services.
- Money flows to me easily and effortlessly.
- I am compensated well for my contributions.
- New opportunities are coming my way easily and effortlessly.

Remember, at the core of you, you are more than what you see in the mirror. You are more than your job. You are more than your desires. You are Source energy and anything is possible. You are the creator of your life and everything you see in it. So create something that feels good! Follow your bliss. It's your spiritual compass.

Chapter 30

Be Authentic

No More Masks—Be Authentic

Being authentic brings you back to presence and when living in presence you can only see your authentic self. Stay present and you are always going to come from an authentic way of living. Living authentically is so pivotal to living an enlightened, happy, joy-filled life. It's key!

Get on with your life now! Stop wasting your time pretending to be something you're not. Be who you are! And live. Stand in your integrity and be the grace that you are. Speaking and living in your truth isn't always going to be easy for many. It can be hard to be conscious of your truth and not go along with mass consciousness as well as social standards. We spend so much time and effort avoiding who we truly are and masking our authentic selves from others and even worse from ourselves. Speaking your truth will not make every one happy but it is your divine course to always be true to yourself first. To be real, that is living life with truth and meaning. . . . to be the real and true YOU is an internal quest. We must rid ourselves of conditions of years past and social expectations. We must listen to our INTERNAL voice and not that of someone else's. It can take lifetimes to conquer this. It is a challenge to remain in our authentic self while still living peacefully with others. We may push a few buttons if another is resisting our true self but we must honor our true selves while remaining as kind and compassionate as we can to those around us.

What's comforting to know is that as you practice being conscious more of being your true authentic self, it becomes easier. An inner glow comes from within and you simply are being authentic no matter what others opinions are. It's as if you have no choice but to show who you truly are. It's liberating and illuminating!

And then we have Zero Point. Zero Point is named differently depending upon who you're talking to. In the Hawaiian clearing method called Ho'oponopono it's getting to Zero or that zero point. Some more quantum folks will use this name as well. It's known as a state of presence by Eckhart Tolle . . . being in that present moment . . . bliss . . . peace . . . getting to a frame of no-thought by others or a connection to total consciousness—Self-realization. The goal is usually to get to Zero point and stick around. Or, for some, go to Zero point and hang out for a bit but be able to still live life here and straddle the line. I like that option. Awakening to the self realized but being in that state of presence that takes away from simple awakening to complete awareness of the self. Mmmm I'm sure you now know it's kind of all one in the same and up to you how you filter it into your system and your way of being. Being authentic is becoming aware of your truest self to the core. A natural progression can get you to your true self.

My heart tells me what I need to do. I share with you that we must stop listening to what others think about us. Stop getting validation from the outside and look within. Every time I look within, I truly feel more validation from

Self . . . mmm . . . even beyond validation to truth and bliss and surrender. And things I don't like are there, but I am doing my best to be truthful about those things too. I know I ignore and resist at times. And as I get these reminders over and over I resist less and less and become more aware, more mindful. Even now I wonder of what you, who are reading this, might think of my inner process and writings. Will it be felt as my truth? It feels like truth at this moment. More surrendering, breathing and being reminds me that it's all divine. No matter what. And so, I breathe.

It's time to live in your truth, integrity and bliss. Be your authentic self. Not what anyone else wants you to be. It's all about your bliss barometer! What makes you feel good is your path to your authentic blissful self. Just because social conditionings have said certain actions or ways of living aren't "normal" doesn't mean it's not a part of YOUR path. You could be one of the few that brings out a better way of living simply by following your bliss barometer. Be open to new possibilities that truly awaken your path to live life to your fullest! Shine your inner light now!

I desire living a life that is spiritual, meaningful, authentic and blissful. One that brings me to the depths of the divine soul itself; a deep spiritual connection.

The things that are most painful to face or hear from another are the very things that are blocking your flow of energy to awakening. Our emotions and body never lie. Become conscious of those feelings and ask what you need to release to be true to yourself. Not listening to your divine self or truth when you hear it, no matter how painful is holding you back from the greatness you are. It's so easy to stay in your own world and only hear what you want to hear. But our shadow side must be faced, processed, embraced and integrated. Beliefs, behaviors, old fears and patterns are so easily rationalized away. You can try to justify it with this excuse and that excuse. But they are just excuses. They are only delaying the inevitable and making it harder for you to come back to yourself.

Don't wait for a certain time period in life. The time is only now. Make it happen, if only a little at a time. I've learned that we have to stay happy with ourselves no matter what we are "waiting" for or whom we are waiting for. But rather simply live as much as we can while processing a challenging experience. And then simply live in our truth, no matter what is going on around us. As you honor your authentic self, your truth, your integrity from within and show it to the world you align more fully to your divine purpose and passions. You see more fully your true essence and what you are meant to offer as your contribution to this reality. And it is simply that: living your authentic true self always while allowing others to do the same thing for themselves and their lives.

For example, some people are living their lives and their careers by what they think their parents or other people expect of them. Following someone else's guidelines of who they should be out of fear of how they might react. So instead of following their passion they are repressing a huge part of themselves in order to follow someone else's expectations of them and make others happy. But are they happy? Many find themselves in deep depression, anger and resentment when following this destructive path. When you wake up to realize you aren't where you want to be anymore or possibly never were, start taking steps to bring yourself back to who you desire being. One step at a time and you will get there. If you don't know who that is, a journal is a great way to get your thoughts down and really see the experiences that led you to where you are and why. This will assist you in moving forward to where you desire being. Be patient with yourself.

Even in writing this book I have been constantly tested to be authentic and truthful in my writing. This book is my learning ground. I have caught myself many times writing what I thought people would like to hear rather than writing from MY HEART and MY AUTHENTIC SELF. So I have deleted a lot of text throughout the writing process of this book, simply because I realized it wasn't me.

Many of us live in a world of gossip, victimhood and drama. And if you're like me, you just don't want to play that part anymore! It's a wise person to start taking responsibility for all actions in their lives that have happened around them. Nothing is happening TO you. You are not a victim. Things simply Are. The art of forgiving yourself and others for experiences you've had may be of benefit when taking back your power. So as much as I can help it, I remove myself from those types of conversations that enable the victim stance and gossiping. If asked my opinion I may nod my head and shrug my shoulders as if to say 'I don't want to share or don't have an opinion'. Or I will simply state my truest opinion of a positive outcome and stating that it's all divine (rare in most circles but I feel each situation out). It's a work in progress even now!

If you can come to a stance of "It's not good. It's not bad. It just is." Then you are in a state of neutrality and allowing the world to work its wonders. Now, if your authentic self is still telling you that you must play a part in whatever drama is happening, that is divine as well. Allow it to flow but always check in with your soul, your truest heart. Ask if this is truly the authentic being you are striving to bring out to the world. If the answer is a resounding NO, then take that strong message from your true self. Do something about it next time the situation comes up or whenever it seems right for you now. Maybe it's simply doing nothing and that is perfectly divine.

Being authentic means no more artificial smiles or self-centered purposes. Pay attention to inner qualities. That is being authentic. Being authentic will not make everyone happy. Those people are feeling uncomfortable in their own skin watching your authentic self. This is their issue. They will get angry and mean or spiteful. Again, stay within your true divine self. It's time. You do not need another's approval in order to follow your dreams and live in your truth. Denise Linn says it best here, "I'm examining ways, within myself, to speak straight from the heart as much as possible in every situation (but in a way that is kind). I have found that when I communicate my truth with joy, clarity and focus (and the willingness to allow folks the opportunity to respond in whatever way feels right to them without judging them for their reaction) my relationships flourish."

Another example is telling the truth. I'm not simply talking about your obvious truths, but the "white lies" people tend to tell themselves and others in order to not be put into a situation they aren't comfortable with. Another mask covers you up. Let's say someone has a gift of service to offer. If the other person doesn't want their services but have a hard time saying no thank you, it gets uncomfortable. They may lead you on and say, "Yes, I'm interested. I'll get back to you" or "Yes, that sounds great. We'll talk soon." This causes negative attachments. When the service is offered again but there is no response back, the person must eventually come to the conclusion that they were blown off. Instead the other person could have spoken their truth and said, "No thank you". Their truth. It is simply what **is**. There is no need to spare feelings, even if the other person would be upset at first. **Your truth can be shared kindly.** It's simply a matter of logistics and the energies not being right for you in that space. It's divine!

Here again music plays a part in giving me a message. A song played in my mind over and over again. Just the chorus: "Say what you need to say" by John Mayer.

It is as simple as what the chorus states. Say what you mean to say. Say what you need to say. Now is the time to say everything that you need to say and what you truly mean to say. It is not the time to beat around the bush or use round-about ways to hopefully say what you mean to say. Speak your truth with kindness; be in your integrity and faith. It is okay to be vulnerable.

In your vulnerability is also your strength. We show that we are human. Humans have weaknesses as you are willing to work on and ask for assistance there is innocence, wisdom and purity. In your vulnerability you are seen as the truest light form you are and others will relate in new levels with your genuine openness. Not to mention that as you embrace your vulnerability you are opening up to know yourself and one another at a greater depth, to realize your true Oneness connection. Thus surrendering to the Divine occurs more easily.

To be in your truth is to be aware of your thoughts and emotions in every moment. Letting them flow in and out. Not repressing them with thoughts of saving them for later. Release these thoughts and emotions in whatever healthy means possible. If you need to write them down, do that. If you need to wait just a few hours for privacy and know then that you will give yourself and your soul time to heal and release.

Even when an answer comes that is uncomfortable, at first, it then turns into a blessing down the road. Even if you never see the blessing in your face, it's still there! So for the person who thought they were being kind by skirting around not wanting to offer an opportunity to another, they were really not listening or operating in their truth and they were then further adding more negative energy by allowing you to feel there was a chance at this opportunity. Instead, speak your truth, state the facts as kindly and compassionately as you can and allow the person to sever those cords and look for more opportunities elsewhere.

I am reminded of the movie *Liar Liar* starring Jim Carey. A hilarious movie that tells it like it is. A little boy makes a birthday wish that for one day his father couldn't tell a lie. The power of the Universe happens and magically this wish comes true. His father, played by Jim Carey, is a lawyer. So you can see the fun that happens here! The lawyer wakes up to the big lies and the little lies he's been telling people for years! Although this is colorfully expressed in the movie there are truths to what is shared. The judgments he internally made of other people come out. He realized the negativity he was spewing in his mind aimed at others. But then a light bulb goes off and he suddenly sees the truth and wants the truth and sees others in an even higher seemingly divine place. Granted this is my viewpoint here so that I can share the point of how being authentic truly is beneficial from the inside out! You notice the mirrors that people have been showing you for years and you realize the nature of being authentic brings you to a higher place of viewing everything as truth and every as divine. A magical landscape is opened up to you as you cross that veil. You cause a shift in your soul when you listen from within and act from your true self.

Being authentic and true to yourself doesn't mean you can't be genuinely kind and take another's feelings into consideration.

218

Remember what you see in another is truly what you are seeing or judging within yourself. So if you see something you don't like, ask yourself what it is in you that you don't like or are judging. See the lessons that are shown. Sometimes there really is no benefit from talking of your beliefs about something. Sometimes the only thing that may occur is more hurt by stating something, so choose non action as your truth. Be the witness. See what lessons this reveals within yourself. Choose wisely while always living in your truth. Sometimes hurt does happen but a truth was to be shared and that is divine. The person or persons hurting will grow from the experiences. It's all in perfect order.

Some people allow peer pressure or what someone else believes to decide for them what they will do or believe. When you listen to the majority or peer pressure and do something you aren't feeling called to do, you are not following your truest path. You will eventually get into a funk, a downward spiral and your resistance to your divine self will eventually manifest as illness in the body! So stay the path.

Yet another example is the desire to move your body. Aside from your responsibilities, if time allows DANCE! Dance like nobodies watching! Simply allow your spirit to unfold naturally. It's so easy to hear the whispers of the few who say that person is "strange" or "weird". But why is it weird to dance or smile while walking down the street. If you're happy why can't you show it!? Why has that become a "weird" trait. I guarantee you, if you start smiling down the street you'll eventually see many people lighting up from the smile you shared with then. Whether you see the shift in them or not, you have played a part in boosting another's demeanor simply by BEING AUTHENTIC!

Live your life as you wish it. Be alive in life. Share your authentic unique self with the world. Really emerge from the cocoon you may be sleeping in and feel the grandeur that you hold within you and allow it to shine out into the world now.

Part of living your authentic self is to allow others the same courtesy. Someone else's truth may not necessarily align with your truth, but that doesn't make them wrong. In that moment this is what they align with and is perfectly "right" for them. Just as with whatever it is that you are BEING in any moment is perfectly right and just for you. It's so easy to go off on a tangent and spout how right you are but sometimes the person listening isn't there in your vibrational space yet. If that is the case their vibration is not going to allow them to see what you are saying or where you are coming from. They simply will not hear you. Or the person listening might actually be on a higher rung than you and you can't see it from your perspective just yet. When you do, you'll say "ah-haa, now I know . . ." As Odo on the television show *Star Trek: Deep Space Nine* says, "They are trapped in a single perspective. They cannot see what's really going on". And this is especially challenging with those you hold dear and as a parent. A divine balance beam is finely walked as much as possible here. There is teaching and there is preaching. You can offer your truth by simply living it and offering kindness along your path. But you don't have to force another to be in your space or your beliefs. They are right with wherever they are.

Be authentic and out yourself. Have a coming out party for yourself! Whether you are eat meat or not; whether you are a Christian, Buddhist or an atheist; whether you are a corporate 9-5'er, musician or gypsy; gay or straight; no matter the path all are divine. All lead paths lead to the same. All paths lead to Source.

We are living in multiple dimensions and ascending at different rates. Someone else might not quite be where you are yet and what they believe in is working for them right now. And again, another may be even more in alignment with a higher way that you aren't quite resonating with yet and that's perfectly divine as well. It's okay to allow others to be right where they are. When it comes time for another to learn something new, to ascend on the ladder of ascension and raise their vibrations, they will come to a new learning or truth. The teacher will be ready for them because they are ready to hear the teacher. When they come asking for your thoughts, then you can share from a neutral peaceful place. As Shiva Rae so gracefully puts it, "The Goddess is my agent. I go where I am invited."

Try to be the witness and simply see each path as divine. Mohandas Gandhi was right when he said if you want positive change, "Be the Change you wish to see in the world." Occasionally a change that you take from an internal yearning feels uncomfortable. This is only temporary. It's a new adventure. You need to give yourself a little time to give it a chance. Don't let the majority be right by law of attraction simply because you don't feel quite comfortable in a new endeavor you thought you wanted. Whatever you believe, the universe will provide you the proof. So believe the highest and best, good of yourself! Give it a little time to adjust in your body, mind and soul. It's can be a little like a bumpy road getting smoother the more you practice this new idea or action. So enjoy aliveness, living and change as long as it is your truth!

When you are authentic, you are in vibrational alignment with your soul! Abraham-Hicks further states, "When you find vibrational alignment with You, you personally thrive. You feel good; you look good; you have stamina; you have energy; you have balance; you have clarity; you have wit; you have abundance of all things that you consider to be good. You thrive in all ways when you come into Energy Balance with You. Vibrational Relativity—that's what it's all about."

Breathing techniques, meditation, exercise and being with nature are profound methods for connecting with your authentic self. These are helpful options to assist in releasing old patterns and reconnecting with the Divine. In your truth with how you feel about situations there is tact involved. But do speak your truth in the moment you feel it as best you can. If the moment is asking you to only speak this truth to yourself that is okay. As you do you will be surprised at the beautiful revelations that flow through you to others and from them to you. As you release with non-judgment you are in the flow. Amazing things open up more easily than before. You feel more at peace with yourself and your life as a whole. You are living in the moment. Breathe and be at peace!

Remember to always check in with yourself to know when your actions are coming from your true authentic being or from your ego. Consistently be conscious of your true self. Your ego is brass, abrupt, impatient, drama-filled, jealous, self-centered, spiteful, and filled with me, me, me, and I, I, I's. Your authentic self is patient, trusting, loving, blissful, and joy-filled! You will feel the difference when you stop, breathe, check in and feel the inner knowing. There is peace in trusting the process. You can gain that deeper connection to that sacred and powerful place inside of you. In truth, integrity and authentic passion your inner fire emerges and shines forth for the world to see.

Chapter 31

I Choose Me

Soul Mates in Ascension—I Choose Me

As a part of living authentically we must start with ourselves and stop chasing someone else to make us "complete". Since we already ARE complete. So it's important to dedicate a little time talking about soul mates.

Would you like to find your Soul Mate? Your one true love? Twin Flame? Whatever name you go by, it still boils down to first being your true self. Love yourself FIRST! Sounds simple, yet we humans tend to get it all mixed up and complicated. I was right there with a lot of people who had this same feeling. That maybe I will feel complete if I had my soul mate by my side. Someone special to share everything with and someone that loves me and shares everything with me as well. Don't get me wrong, this is actually a great thing to desire and also gets us closer to the Divine by being in that vibration. Being open to love in this realm opens our heart to God even more, which is why we have these experiences. However, in combination with this desire we must be sure we are going along our merry little way following our very own passions and joys. Find your soul mate? Sure! Do something YOU love and as you go along your way you will naturally attract that person to you. God provides that which you are beaming out to the world. Surrender to ever finding that special someone. Surrender ever needing them. We don't need them. What we desire is a love connection found only within.

Susyn with www.kajama.com encapsulates this thought, "Master the art of keeping your focus on yourself, it will be easier to manifest fulfillment. The more you focus on yourself, the more you'll glow with spiritual light, and then you'll attract a soul mate like a moth to a flame. Good luck on your search for true love!"

Now, do Soul Mates exist? You bet. But it may or may not be in the meaning that you give the name. I used to believe in the notion of the one and only special partner that was only meant for me and me for them. This still may be true for some or some on different levels of reality. And now I believe all relationships are divine and progress into more beautiful expressions each time. I may be with my one and only Soul Mate now under this new belief. However, I know that the Universe is funny and constantly changing and evolving. So I am simply embracing the present living in the moment with my beloved Husband.

This need or desire for a Soul Mate may stem from before birth. Prior to incarnating we had an unconditionally loving connection to the Divine beyond all that we can comprehend in our 3D reality. This connection was then stripped from our memories when we incarnated so that we can go through the lessons that we are required to process in this lifetime. However, we still strive for that ultimate connection. Oneness. We look for it with our soul mates, friends and family. It is a built in desire beyond words. This love we strive to share and feel is the ultimate radiance. And for brief moments of time in relationships we will feel something that comes close to that connected feeling. But this is surface satisfaction. It then dissipates and we again search out the next "high" to get us to that beautiful feeling again. It is not wrong. It simply is.

Knowing this we can start a process of wisely diving deeper within. Now, we can feel our divine connection from within and someday upon full enlightenment we can embody the All That Is. We are not separate, it is just an illusion we are born into. As we remember this truth from deep within our soul we will stop looking for love outside of ourselves and feel that which was always there from within. We are Source and Source is us.

I'm embracing more the belief that a "Soul Mate" is not just your one and only truly devoted other half, at least not in this dimension. That name goes to your Twin Flame. It is believed by many that your Twin Flame is not someone that is incarnated here in the same life with you. Instead, they are lovingly supporting you always from the Other Side (Heaven if you will). They are your perfect match and reside by your side in the realms of spirit. You reunite once you have completed your mission here on Earth. Now Soul Mates fall under a new definition. I believe it is possible that we have many Soul Mates in one lifetime. Now this is *not* true for everyone. We each have our own individual lessons and karma that runs its course in our lives. Some people are lucky to have only one and others are lucky to have maybe up to five truly devoted other halves in this incarnation. That is to say that at the time you are with this person they are your match vibrationally and are with you for certain lessons. You may or may not, by the law of free will, choose to be with this person for a long period of time. Sometimes you are meant to go your separate ways and meet another who is even more your match now as your vibrations have naturally evolved into something new. A natural progression may ensue for some of us. Where you are with one soul mate in a certain pattern and then when you have released that old past pattern with this soul mate you are able to move forward away from said soul mate and be with yourself.

Then sooner or later a new soul mate comes to you with new lessons to learn and evolve from.

These soul mates can be past life partners as well. So a strong connection can be felt from the cellular level as you remember in your soul knowing this person before. You may remember the agreement made in spirit to be with this person for a time to learn a few lessons and then move on. There is no one way to believe; no one way to go with this scenario. We are each unique and have our unique challenges to go through. My advice would be to enjoy the person you are with immensely as they are and enjoy expressing your authentic self with them and everyone you come in contact with.

I used to have my desires in the wrong order. I thought number one: Find Soul Mate, number two: Be Happy. In my evolvement I've learned that it's 100% the other way around!! BE HAPPY FIRST! Then you will attract all you desire and more. Because you are a vibrational match for what you receive it makes sense that if you are happy and love yourself you will receive a relationship that is happy and loving at that deep level.

What had to happen for me was I had to start turning down the first person who showed interest. I had to find and follow my joys and passions first and foremost. (And still do!) I started doing things I enjoy more and more and really enjoy spending time with MYSELF. I love my alone time!! I would read, go out to restaurants that I enjoyed, take classes I love, watch movies I like, order take out, whatever! Outside of loving spending time with my son, I enjoyed reading and going to the beach at night by myself, meditating, energy healing, teaching metaphysical classes. I found out that I really love ME! I love what I love, I love who I became and I still love who I am becoming. I forgave myself for many things I continuously guilted over for many years. I found out that in loving myself, I loved the world! I enjoy JOY!

Remember you do not have to first give to others and then to yourself. That's backwards. You must first be in balance with giving to yourself. There must be balance in giving and receiving. If you are giving too much of yourself to others, you do not have time to give to yourself. Suddenly your life will not only be NOT what you want, but you will notice depression kicking in, health problems and negative experiences continuously creeping in. But you can change that and you can do it right now. You can make that decision to follow YOUR true soul's path. Your destiny is to be happy now for yourself and show others how it's done. They will learn by your example. We all deserve to be happy now, not later. We only have right now.

We're not meant to suffer until we meet that special someone. Or to suffer until we get that perfect job or experience. We're meant to live the life we have now and enjoy it, while creating the best out of what more we desire to enjoy. To follow our excitement and passion!! Only then do we let go enough for things to just easily flow into our lives, like that special someone.

Do what YOU love and enjoy now. If, that is at first, starting small, do that. Sign yourself up for that sewing class, yoga class or night out with your friends that you've been holding off on. Just GO FOR IT. Change your routine and do something you love. Give yourself a new affirmation today: "I am willing to change." Say it daily or many times a day! Change is ever constant, so enjoy it!

If you are already with your Soul Mate, that's awesome! Remember to always be true to you no matter what. Whether you are with your soul mate or not. Always follow your true path. Sometimes it will take you and your soul mate apart and sometimes you grow together. Sometimes the relationship ends sooner than you think, but it doesn't mean that it wasn't meant to be for that time you had with them. There will be gem's you will always take with you from the relationship. You two grew together, even if it took you apart from each other. But always following your true self is prudent. If you are meant to be together for the long haul then you should have no issues being and feeling true to yourself always. If you can't do this, communicate with each other truthfully. See if there is common ground. If there is not, you two can be happy and content with yourselves knowing it is time to depart and start a new journey elsewhere. But know even if that happens, you will always be happy as long as you follow your inner joy.

It's important that when you have found your Soul Mate that you do your best not to get caught up in them. Don't expect them to bring you happiness and fulfillment. If they do that is always nice. But when they don't and you get disappointed you've suddenly given away all your power to those expectations from another. Remember, they are human too and will not be perfect. The idea is to grow together in a strong relationship built on love, trust, happiness and honesty. There will be challenges but you have the core of your being from within that brings you true fulfillment. This can be shared once reached from within. Never rely on another for happiness.

In times past, I have caught myself. I sometimes catch myself doing it again and then "sever" another negative ego cord that I kept expecting something more from another when it's only within ME to make me the HAPPIEST person ever. We don't have to bare THEIR crosses either. Whatever is their stuff is THEIRS and we can be there as a support (but separate from their lessons none-the-less). We only have what is "ours" and can assist when we feel drawn in a detached yet compassionate way with the love we have for them. PHEW! From here it is nice to remember that what we see in them is within us too. So choose wisely how you view your partner, your children, your family, you co-workers and the world.

First and foremost, listen to **your** heart. Honor your desires. Your inner being pulls you to the thing that drives you most. Whatever feels exciting truly IS the path for you. Your soul will give you a "yes" or a "no" feeling towards what you love most. And a lovely woman just told me a few days ago: "If it's not a HELL YES, then it's a 'Hell no'!" If you don't feel it to the core of your being, then don't do it. But if every fiber of your being is screaming with excitement, joy and love it's safe to say you can run in that wonderful direction!

> ". . . When you have the courage to share your vulnerabilities with others, you create a more intimate connection. Being vulnerable allows others to see the

real you that lies beneath any masks you may wear. By letting someone see your weaknesses, as well as your strengths, you allow them to see who you really are. Rather than making you defenseless, your vulnerability demonstrates a courage and openness that can help your relationships flourish."
~ Madisyn Taylor, www.DailyOm.com

Now on to the fun stuff:

- Let people see the REAL you! For if you are not truthful with yourself and others then you are hiding something and it will eventually reveal itself. Be true and open. This goes back to being authentic, as clarified in chapter thirty.
- Life is a mirror. All that is around you is a reflection of what you are thinking, being and vibrating at. We receive a matching frequency of what we are in vibrational alignment with. So send out those vibes of LOVE for yourself and others. See the wonderful beauty in YOU and reflect that goodness to everything you come in contact with.
- Manifest the partner you desire! Make a list of all the things you'd love to enjoy in your perfect mate. Leave room for the Universe to work its magic in the details. Then sit back and visualize this love. You can visualize away! See yourself happy, content, filled with love and compassion for your partner and that person for you! Visualize feeling the highest love. Visualize good times, vacations, family, etc. Enjoy it! Truly FEEL these emotions. In our emotions is the magic to bring miracles. Feel positive love and bring it to you.
- Yes, you should still live in the moment and follow your inner joys NOW! Living in the now and putting desires out for the future are definitely okay as long as you aren't dwelling or falling into

self-pity if it doesn't happen in the time you'd prefer.

- Make these manifesting moments your happy moments a few minutes a day.
- Then let go and let God as they say! Just let it go, surrender to the outcome completely and know the Universe is working out the magical kinks and delivering your package at just the right time.

Your very asking tells you it's in the works. So manifest away! We attract that which we align with. So align with feeling LOVE in every moment. Align with true positive uplifting energy and it comes to you easily. You desire the perfect love, so feel it NOW for yourself and those around you. Put it out there for that matching vibration to come back as you FEEL it and it will be so in the right time for the highest and best, good! ☺

Suddenly, one day while enjoying life my soul mate came to me. All while I wasn't even looking. I knew the moment I met him we'd be married. All because he and I had followed our truest paths, grew into ourselves first and were then and now in vibrational alignment with each other to have an awesome life we create together!

Start with yourself! Do what I did. Know you deserve complete happiness, love and joy! I chose me and I still choose me!

Chapter 32

Laugh

Have a Sense of Humor

Lighten up. 9 Having a sense of human places you in a happy state of mind, as well as a detached state of mind. Detached from worry and fear. Detached from anything that requires further "obligation" into the ego path. Remembering that we are supposed to enjoy life, even during challenging times, can help us truly stay in the Now, the present moment and truly laugh with lightness at all the silliness around.

It can be challenging to laugh at yourself, but having a sense of humility and joy about whatever it is that has happened is truly liberating. You might be talking to a group of friends or in front of a large crowd and suddenly you do something that truly turns your face red. You've either said something incorrectly or improperly or you've tripped while walking and talking and fell flat on your face. That's okay. That's perfect. That's divine. Accepting this by laughing at yourself shows those around you that you are human and it's okay to have vulnerabilities. You truly come off more powerful in being authentically humble and laughing it off.

It's also a challenge, at times, to take with stride the funny things that keep happening to delay a meeting or event you are going to. See these interruptions as the Divine's funny way of showing you timing is everything and that being late isn't always a bad thing. Not only that, you may have avoided a more serious issue if you had been on time. Simply laugh it off. You might even find yourself laughing so much at all the things that keep you from getting to an event on time that your belly hurts! You've let go of controlling situations and simply allowed it to be there. God does have a sense of humor.

Laughter truly is the best medicine! We need humor and laughter as a way of releasing all of the suffering in our world and others. It truly lightens the load, so to speak! I read years ago of a man who was diagnosed with terminal cancel. He locked himself in his room for a week and watched the funniest movies he loved so much—the Three Stooges. After that fun week of laughter, he was cancer free!!! That is AMAZING! Just by letting loose and having some fun he cured an illness that was going to kill his physical body. It's quite possible he hadn't laughed that hard in years and was living a stress-filled life. His body was speaking to him loud and clear. Thank God he listened and laughed!

As you take the stance of not taking things so seriously, not attaching yourself to other peoples circumstances or illusions of worry, you realize that you don't need to be in a huff about life, about challenges. Your life is stress-free. You are more relaxed and peaceful. Then you don't feed more anguish and fear into situations or illusions. Then you don't manifest even more illusions of fear, creating more experiences that spiral into more fear. You instead create more happy moments as you stay in the happy state of mind. You are free. Free to Be.

Chapter 33

Daily Devotion

A long with working on your personal issues with truth and integrity I recommend a daily spiritual practice. I recommend that this practice include meditation and some sort of spiritual movement such as Yoga or even walking. The practice I include in Book Two *Divine Embrace* is also my recommendation as a practice you may choose to utilize. Choose what resonates with you most. But make it a conscious daily practice. Even when you are not in devotion be sure you are consciously in spiritual connection with the Self. To be in this state no matter what you are doing is something you can achieve.

With a daily spiritual practice you will have a balanced soothing awakening. We do know that the Earth is going through a transition right now and is ascending. We also know that we are receiving a constant infusion of energy due to the planetary ascension and the rise of spiritual energy from millions of aspirants across the globe. This in combination with your daily practice will enhance your benefits of coming back to your true Divine self.

Embrace your divine self daily with the tools I've given you here and will also give you in Book Two *Divine Embrace* and modify it to fit YOU! We are each unique and will resonate with many different things at different points in our lives. What you enjoy most is what you should do now!

Now if you also seek out shaktipat, satsang (group energy practice), or other uplifting options you may notice a peek in your energy. And this may prelude to a dip in your energy to a place where you might have been prior to the spiritual awakening energy you received. However, these highs and lows, peaks and valleys, may not be as defined if you have a daily spiritual practice. So when you step out of the spiritual awakening energy of a master or guru you will not dip into the depths of fire nearly as much, if at all, if you have a balanced daily spiritual practice of your own.

In time you will feel a balanced progression and peace no matter where you are or what you are doing. It will be common for you to be in bliss at work, home, the mall, doing yoga, meditation, or nothing at all. You may experience some challenges but again its emphasis is reduced and it's easier to work through the lessons. Because you have a daily practice you are gradually getting to a higher spiritual awakening in a self-paced manner. You are contributing to your own awakening daily. It is a conscious free will choice how you choose to get there; either harshly with upheaval at every turn or smooth and blissful.

So I suggest you take all of the guidelines I've laid out for you as your reference to leading a life of True Inner Peace daily. Follow the divine guidance you receive, as you will receive your own internal guidance if you listen. And take inspired action on this guidance. Get up and move, meditate, use breath awareness, ground, detox your body, think before reacting, forgive, be grateful, live in the present moment, get out in nature, choose wisely, allow others their experiences, come to a place of neutrality and know the Divine knows best. Love yourself. Come back to your heart and have a daily dedicated spiritual practice to the Divinity of your choice. You get the idea. 9 Most of all just Be. Feel the connection. We are always connected. We are the Divine.

*   *   *

No matter what is going on around you, you can be the peace you wish to see in the world. It's not what you see that is going on around you that matters. It's what you feel on the inside. So feel the inner peace that is always there. Remember that there is that place within you that always remains untouched no matter what happens to you in your life. You can feel that peace in any situation. Focus and allow the peace to emulate through you and to the world.

Saint Theresa's Prayer

May today there be peace within.
May you trust God that you are exactly where you are meant to be.
May you not forget the infinite possibilities that are born of faith.
May you use those gifts that you have received, and pass on the love that has been given to you.
May you be content knowing you are a child of God.
Let this presence settle into your bones, and allow your soul the freedom to sing, dance, praise and love.
It is there for each and every one of us.

Afterword

We all desire ultimate unity. We all yearn for our utopia, our Bali, our heaven on Earth. The more we feel it and be it, the more we are it. In Bali they respect each other to high standards, bowing to each other with grace and love. No matter who you are, love and grace flows to you. This I strive for every day more and more. As I bring more loving ways of being and feeling, I allow more conscious awareness to flow from me to another naturally. When I am in that place in me, I know I am that person from within. It is my sincerest wish that the magic of the Divine embraces you as the Divine continues to embrace me. Allow and enjoy!

May you always know the peace that dwells within. My path is to awaken, empower and motivate individuals along their path. I offer a part of me to you in this book. I offer information and only one of many ways to reach the same goal. I know that as I evolve my opinions and way of being will evolve and change. So, too, will the way I view life. We are all ascending to a new higher dimension. As we do this our ego filter dissolves and falls away. As this happens one drop at a time, we see a new level of awareness before us and within us. Utter bliss is upon each and every one of us. Allow and surrender to the Divine.

There are many paths and they all lead to the same. In the end whatever path we take is the Divine right path for us as individuals. We are all uniquely different and will do things even slightly different than everyone else. Dance with life in YOUR way, not someone else's. It is nice to hear of a path that worked for someone else and see if even part of it will work for you. If you get that twinge in your gut of excitement, energy or love then that is right for you. If you only take bits and pieces of this book with you on your path, then that is perfect and divine for you. Take whatever resonates with you and leave all the rest. Some of the information may pose as a seed to be planted and other pieces of this book may not resonate. But with an open mind and heart you will reach your goal in whatever way you are meant to and in whatever way you are most comfortable doing. Enjoy the ride. Relax. The ride does not have to be uncomfortable. It is not about the end result, as much as it is about enjoying the ride as you get there! Bliss to you! And as always, follow your bliss! It's your Spiritual Compass.

References

I'd like to thank the following people for their beautiful information and quotes that really assisted in driving home points of reference:

- Mother Theresa
- Abraham-Hicks, Abraham-Hicks.com
- Chalene Johnson, *Turbo Jam,* TurboJam.com
- Denise Austin, DeniseAustin.com
- Anthony Robbins, www.tonyrobbins.com
- Jack Hawley, Bhagavad Gita: A Walkthrough for Westerners
- Dr. Zhi Gang Sha, PowerofSoul.com and SoulMastersMovie.com
- Gurumayi Chidvilasananda, SiddhaYoga.org
- Buddha
- *What the Bleep do we Know!?,* WhatTheBleep.com
- Denise Linn, *Feng Shui for the Soul* and *Space Clearing A-Z: How to Use Feng Shui to Purify and Bless Your Home* both
- Dawn, LovesGuidingLight.com
- Matt Kahn, TrueDivineNature.com
- Madisyn Taylor, DailyOm.com
- Eckhart Tolle, *A New Earth*
- *Next,* IMDB.com/title/tt0435705/
- Dr. Wayne Dyer, DrWayneDyer.com
- Cynthia Sue Larson, RealityShifters.com
- Mike Dooley, *Notes from the Universe,* Tut.com
- Doreen Virtue, *Divine Magic* and *Angel Numbers 101*
- Coast to Coast AM Radio Show, CoasttoCoastam.com
- Star Wars, StarWars.com

- Oprah Winfrey, <u>Oprah.com</u>
- 3 Doors Down, *It's not my time*
- Mohandas Gandhi, *Gandhi, An Autobiography*
- Dr. Phil, *Dr. Phil Show*
- Yvonne Kason, *Farther Shores*
- Osho, *The Book of Secrets*
- Alanis Morrisette, *Everything*
- Tom Kenyon channeling The Hathors, <u>TomKenyon.com</u>
- Albert Einstein
- T.K.V. Desikachar, Heart of Yoga
- Linda Jaros, <u>TheLifeBreathInstitute.com</u>, and Dr. Tom Good, <u>InternationalBreathInstitute.com</u>
- Gerd Lange
- Sondra Ray, *Rock your world with the Divine Mother and How to be Chic, Fab and Live Forever*, <u>SondraRay.com</u>
- Joseph Campbell
- Kim Marcille Romaner, *The Science of Making Things Happen*
- Matt Kahn, <u>TrueDivineNature.com</u>
- Swami Muktananda
- Bertrand Russell, *Unpopular Essays*
- Dr. Carl Jung
- Mike George, <u>Relax7.com</u>
- Dalai Lama
- R. Brash, *How Did It Begin: A fascinating study of the superstitions, customs, and strange habits that influence our daily lives*
- Corita Kent
- Deepak Chopra
- Chrism, <u>KundaliniAwakeningSystems1.com</u>
- John Mayer, *Say what you need to say*
- Odo character, *Star Trek: Deep Space Nine*
- Shiva Rae, <u>ShivaRae.com</u>
- Catherine Ponder, <u>CatherinePonder.wwwhubs.com</u>
- Saint Theresa

About the Author

Maggie Anderson, CYT, RMT, CSC & CPLC

Yoga Instructor, Reiki Master Teacher, Spiritual Teacher, Soul Coach
SpiritualCompassConnection.com
MaggieAnderson7@yahoo.com

Maggie's passion resides in offering Yoga instruction, a variety of Spiritual Classes, Soul Coaching, and Energy Healing Sessions all while assisting each soul find & follow their truest passion in awakening. Giving you the tools that help *you* get and stay inspired. The power is within us. Trained in numerous Healing arts, Maggie's desire is to work with individuals in increasing their Divine connection during these Ascension times, and thereby increasing peace, harmony & flow. She lights up when she sees the spark in another awaken. Maggie works as the channel for you to open up to who you've always been. To open up to your full Power. To Awaken.

Maggie offers a variety of classes including: Yoga, 28-Day Soul Coaching Program, Thinner Lighter Healthier You (manifesting the body you desire), Divine Embrace, True Inner Peace, Kundalini & Ascension, Space Clearing for a Peaceful Home and more. Maggie's writings have been published in a variety of publications. She resides in Cumberland, RI.

If you'd like to learn more about awakening and embracing your true Divine Self, as well as sign up for Maggie's free newsletter please visit her Web Site at: www.SpiritualCompassConnection.com.

Sat
April 26

CPSIA information can be obtained at www.ICGtesting.com
Printed in the USA
BVOW021244290911

272394BV00001B/7/P

9 781452 538242